THE STRIP & FLIP SELECTION OF 2016
Five Jim Crows & Electronic Election Theft

Bob Fitrakis & Harvey Wasserman

Introduced by Greg Palast and Mimi Kennedy

CICJ BOOKS
Columbus, Ohio

THE STRIP & FLIP SELECTION OF 2016
Five Jim Crows & Electronic Election Theft

Copyright ©2016
Bob Fitrakis & Harvey Wasserman
All Rights Reserved

2016 paperback printing
ISBN: 978-1-62249-336-4

Cover art by John Bailey.
Publisheed in the United States of America by CICJ Books
Columbus Institute for Contemporary Journalism,
a 501(c)(3) nonprofit organization
1021 E. Broad Street, Columbus Ohio 43205
www.freepress.org
www.solartopia.org

Printed by Zip Publishing
1313 Chesapeake Ave., Columbus, Ohio 43212
The Educational Publisher
www.EduPublisher.com

Acknowledgements

This compendium could not have happened without the tireless work of Suzanne Patzer, who took the brunt of a very difficult job. Pete Johnson and Kirk Bampton did extensive proofreading. Mimi Kennedy, Greg Palast and innumerable other stalwart election protection activists continue to defend what's left of our democracy. We are also heavily indebted to mathematician Richard Charnin, not only for his clear and concise analysis of election rigging and thank him for the use of his charts and graphs in this book. We've been working with the illustrator John Bailey for more than two decades and we appreciate his enduring ability to always graphically capture our ideas behind our words. And a special thanks to *Columbus Free Press* graphic artist Crystal Dawn O'Donovan who laid it out and turned it into a book. We hope this small compendium will make a difference.

Table of Contents

Strip and Flip: Preface by Greg Palast   1

Introduction by Mimi Kennedy   4

Prologue   7

PART ONE: "STRIP"   15

The First Jim Crow: Slavery and the 3/5ths Clause   19

The Second Jim Crow: American Apartheid   23

The Third Jim Crow: The Drug War   29

PART TWO: "FLIP"

The Fourth Jim Crow: Election Theft Goes Global   40

The Fifth Jim Crow: Election Theft Comes To The US   54

Strip and Flip: Preface
By Greg Palast

There's something really, really weird about Bob Fitrakis and Harvey Wasserman.

Sensible Americans were doing everything in their power this summer to avoid all thought of the Presidential election, its icky choices, its barf-making ads, the chatter-heads and chuckle-heads on TV spewing brain-cell killing bromides and the parade of officious ponces who call themselves "elected officials" and the wannabe electeds – while Bob and Harvey worked like dogs to protect Our Democracy.

Are they delusional schmucks? Heroic heralds of the death of our freedoms? Two guys with oozing envy of billionaires and their trophy senators? Paul Reveres of the internet screeching, *They're stealing your vote! They're stealing your vote!?*

Like the investigations in *"Strip and Flip,"* I am once again knocked over by the authors' erudition, authoritative analysis, stunning and ill-making revelations and irrefutable evidence of a national emergency: Grand Theft Election.

Attorney and political science professor Fitrakis and historian Wasserman know their stuff – and you should know it too.

I've been in the election theft biz a long time - that is, reporting on the schemers and scammers who jack with your ballot, your registration and your government. It started in 2000 when Al Gore was down for the count against George W. Bush and I got my hands on a set of computer disks from the office of the Secretary of State of Florida, Katherine Harris. Harris had tagged 94,000 citizens for removal from the voter rolls. She called them, "felons," but every one, I mean *every one*, was innocent, though most were guilty of VWB: Voting While Black.

That's when I encountered Professors Fitrakis' and Wasserman's first work into the too-many ways in which ballot bandits can eliminate your registration, hang your chad and throw your vote into the garbage-sometimes legally, sometimes not, but always, always, stealing away the last power-voting-of the poor, the dark-skinned, the young and the learned (students get dicked around a lot at polling places).

Vote theft is class war by other means

The Country Club set are none too tolerant of sharing ballot boxes with voters of color, students and the unemployed. The billionaires understand well that the victims of their financial machinations may not vote as told. The un-privileged are not voters to convince but as voters to blockade. The rich guys' weapons include crazy ID requirements – and, of course, more felon purges. (Fitrakis and Wasserman uncover Ohio's purge of felon voters from registries - although ex-cons are allowed to vote in Ohio!)

Indeed, historian Wasserman is quick to lay out the sordid history of vote theft by the Democratic Party (it was the Democrats who came up with the original Jim Crow laws removing "felons" from voter rolls). I have to say I was shocked (that does not happen often) to read here about the number of elections, *beginning with Thomas Jefferson's*, bent by a crooked voting system.

I am flattered and chuffed (a British-ism - you can look it up) to find my own investigative findings in Part II, The Sixth Jim Crow. Every bullet point wins you a bet against your dumb uncle who swears by Rush. Did you know that in the last Presidential elections, one and a half *million* ballots were "spoiled," not counted – that's official – and 54% of those tossed ballots were cast by African-Americans? Well, now you do.

So, what are you going to do about it?

First, you're going to read this book, then you're going to go to www. FreePress.org to get the latest from these searchers for truth.

This book, this new Civil Rights Movement, is not about stopping Republicans from winning office – hell, go and vote for Trumpty-Dumpty or a Clinstone-like, *whatever*. This book is about stopping *vote theft*.

One of my heroes is US Navy Captain David Iglesias, former US Attorney for New Mexico. Iglesias, one of the models for the Tom Cruise character in *A Few Good Men*, is a stalwart Republican who wants his party to win elections. But what he doesn't want is for his party to steal elections - and that is what Karl Rove, Senior Counsel to then-President George Bush, wanted him to do. When the Captain wouldn't go along with phony arrests of "fraudulent" voters, Rove had Bush fire Iglesias.

Captain Iglesias was not standing up for Democrats, but for *democracy*. To Iglesias, and to Fitrakis and Wasserman, the future of our imperiled democracy is worth their blood, sweat, tears and toil. And now we need yours.

This book's title, *The Strip & Flip Selection of 2016: Five Jim Crows and Electronic Election Theft* is a challenge... for you. It's up to you to prevent theft. Get informed, then put on a badge. If you don't join the Democracy posse, who will?

Greg Palast has reported on elections theft for BBC Television London, The Guardian, Harper's, Rolling Stone, and The Nation.

Palast's film, The Best Democracy Money Can Buy: A Tale of Billionaires & Ballot Bandits, based on his bestselling books, will be released before the 2016 election.
Info at www.GregPalast.com.

Palast book, which includes a 48-page comic book by Ted Rall, is **Billionaires & Ballot Bandits: How to Steal an Election in 9 Easy Steps.** It will be released on September 18. For more info, go to: www.BallotBandits.org.

Introduction
By Mimi Kennedy

W hen I was young, I loved politics. Campaigns were fun and Election Day honest and decisive. When Eisenhower defeated Adlai Stevenson I considered it the inevitable, happy outcome of "I Like Ike" buttons predominating in my neighborhood – which was middle class and white.

My father was a Republican lawyer and very involved in elections. I remember one morning after Election Day he came down to breakfast bleary-eyed, having come in late the night before, and my mother asked him why. "The margin," he replied with a nervous chuckle, "was very thin."

I remember wondering why that mattered.

I remember going door-to-door with him to get out the vote. Once, he knocked on a door softly, then turned away, though he'd been more adamant elsewhere. "I don't have to try too hard there," he explained. "I think Ed's a Democrat." He seemed a little abashed, and I credit him now with not having wanted to reveal the venality of preference in this patriotic activity. As a lawyer, he'd always insisted on equality under the law. We didn't judge, in the United States, according to race, color or creed. But on Election Day, it seemed, things were a little different. Some voters were more valuable than others.

Those days seem quaint to me now. It's 2016, and preference is boasted of, not apologized for. Big Data has massively enabled it, from digital registration rolls to digital vote-casting and counting.

But computer code is unreadable to most citizens, so if results don't seem right to the public, there's little we can do about it except hire experts and lawyers to file for recounts and court challenges. Electronic election fraud goes back to the CIA's use of it on behalf of preferred dictator Ferdinand Marcos in the Phillippines – a fact I learned from Wasserman and Fitrakis. And by now it's an almost perfect crime.

In November 2000, I watched the NAACP hearings held in Dade County, Florida. African American residents lined up to testify about their experiences on Election Day. You can still watch it here in the C-SPAN archives: http://www.c-span.org/video/?160466-1/voting-problems-florida. I recommend it.

Those hearings are horrifying. And the reason Wasserman and Fitrakis identify electronic election theft as the Fifth Jim Crow is that little has changed except the proliferation of easier, less risky means to accomplish the goal of preferring certain votes, and discouraging others, in any race. In Florida, while Dade County African Americans told of suppression, Katherine Harris, their white Secretary of State, boasted of her good election whose results would soon be certified. Bush was ahead by about 350 votes. A very thin margin indeed, though she'd overseen a purge of 94,000 mostly African American voters from Florida rolls before Election Day.

In 2004, Ohio decided Bush's re-election. And the Secretary of State – again a co-chair of Bush's campaign in the state – was African-American, J. Kenneth Blackwell. Jim Crow had become Equal Opportunity.

What had happened between 2000 and 2004 was the Help America Vote Act. Meant to correct problems with Florida paper punch-card ballots, it was fraud capacity disguised as reform. It encouraged the buying of electronic voting systems as the solution to federal mandates. The hope that true reformists had was that computers would prove colorblind.

Instead, computer counting made us blind. We no longer see our votes being counted. As in any darkness, nefarious schemes are much easier to accomplish.

African Americans are still the target of suppression schemes. They've been joined by young people who question authority and the status quo; immigrants, and others whose votes are not preferred as reliably loyal to whomever uses fraud to seize power.

Bigotry plus technology has noosed us. Without paper ballots, our votes can't be counted publicly, election results are not verifiable. Yet intentional manipulation of the errors we see increasingly is almost impossible to prove. Elections are almost impossible to reverse. They're expensive to run the first time, let alone again and again. Though we suspect problems when election results are weird, we have no idea how to prove they're wrong – or solve them before the next election.

This will change. Wasserman and Fitrakis show us the way. Some solutions will take time. Meanwhile, letting our election officials know we're watching is a first step. Tell them we're interested in how our votes are being counted. If, like me, you loved elections when you were younger, restore your interest and enthusiasm! Don't just cast your vote – help others to the polls and then watch how the votes are counted! There are over 7000 small voting jurisdictions in the U.S., with different voting systems and different customs and procedures. Learn yours.

I have called election fraud "The Crime That Dare Not Speak Its Name" – a term coined by Oscar Wilde for homosexuality at the turn of the century. Even our elected officials whose jobs depend on the ballot box seem suspiciously unconcerned about its vulnerability to hacking by friend or foe. They must be concerned. We all must be. So thank Wasserman and Fitrakis for having done it again: laid it all out for us, told us what's happening.

Read it and weep. Mourn – then organize!

THE STRIP & FLIP SELECTION OF 2016
Five Jim Crows & Electronic Election Theft

Prologue

Unless something is done, the next president of the United States will be selected by a tiny handful of politicians and high-tech hackers who control the nation's electronic poll books and voting machines.

They'll also determine who runs the US Congress, judiciary, state and local governments.

The only votes that will really count in 2016 may be those manipulated by partisan computer hackers and the corporate rich who hire them.

Nearly all citizens wishing to vote must hope their names appear on computerized poll books from which millions of legitimate voters are being stripped as you read this.

More than 80% of those who do survive the de-registration process will vote on corporate-owned electronic machines with no paper trail or independent verification.

In 2016, the process gives the Republican Party a strong edge.

Swing states Florida, North Carolina, Ohio, Michigan, Iowa and Arizona all have GOP governors and secretaries of state. With a few keystrokes they can shape the electorate and manipulate the vote count.

Such manipulation is a bi-partisan affair, open to use by the Democrats as well as the GOP.

This book provides a brief history of the two historic keys to controlling our government: the "divide and conquer" use of race and electronic manipulation of our elections.

This book provides a brief history of electronic election theft. We examine what is poised to happen in 2016, and ways it can be stopped.

The "strip and flip" technique of controlling electronic elections can easily apply to citizens of all faiths and color.

But in the US, race has been the critical tool for dividing the populace. It's the bottom-line basic instrument that makes electronic election theft possible.

So we begin with a brief history of four "Jim Crows" of racial assault that have set the stage for the fifth – the electronic theft of 2016 and all future "selections" of candidates in service of the large corporations that increasingly own and operate our government.

Because there's so much compacted information involved, we've formatted this presentation as a succession of succinct critical realities. We hope that makes it all easier to read, understand...and act upon. It's our intent that this presentation be used for public education and organizing.

Unless true accountability is established in our voter registration rolls and electronic vote counts, 2016 could mark the final electronic burial for whatever shreds of American democracy still remain.

So we start with three basic sets of recommendations for action: The "Ohio Plan" to build a foundation for elections that are fair, open and verifiable; "Reshaping Our Democracy" with four large long-term goals; and "An Action Plan for 2016."

We follow with the "Strip" section of our history, outlining the use of race and the Drug War to warp our electoral process. We finish with the "Flip" section, describing the overseas intervention and the origin, use and current state of electronic election theft.

This compendium is meant to be a tool for understanding and teaching the basics of how our electoral system was born corrupt, and has since become a wholly owned subsidiary of the global corporate 1%.

It's essentially unconcerned with producing a flowing narrative or a pleasant read.

It means instead to provide a collection of facts that might be useful in grasping the depth of the "strip and conquer" tactics used to control our body politic, followed by the electronic "flip and steal" methods of massaging and corrupting the vote count where stripping and disenfranchisement have come up short.

As we approach the 2016 election, we fear yet another fiasco aimed at rendering our grassroots nation powerless amidst the worsening realities of social injustice, perpetual war and ecological catastrophe.

We hope this compendium helps empower a grassroots movement that must ultimately take control of our electoral system.

We know that there are many who have no problem believing that undemocratic forces are disenfranchising and suppressing voters but refuse to believe that private, partisan for-profit companies would tamper with the vote that they secretly control through computerized voting machines.

If you have any questions, comments, criticisms, suggestions or otherwise just want to communicate, please contact us at truth@ freepress.org and harvey@freepress.org.

Three sets of recommendations for action:

1. The "Ohio Plan" to Reshape our Elections:

- Voter registration must be universal and automatic for all citizens as they turn 18.
- Electronic poll books are banned, with all voter registration records maintained manually.
- All elections happen over a 4-day weekend in November – Saturday, Sunday, Monday, Tuesday – which together comprise a national holiday ending on our traditional voting day.
- All voting happens on paper ballots, using recycled or hemp paper, to be preserved at least two years.
- All vote counting is done manually, in open public view.
- Polls are run and ballots are counted by the nation's high school and college students, who will get the days off and be paid a "scholarship" for their work at $15/hour.

2. Long-Term Reform of the Election Process:

- Ban corporate money from the campaign process.
- Abolish the Electoral College.

- End gerrymandering.
- Provide free public media access for all candidates meeting certain universal basic requirements.

3. Election Protection 2016:
Threats to the Primary Election Vote and Actions for Activists

Recommendation #1: Monitor all directives and advisories from Secretary of State's office (or highest state election official)

State election officials often attempt to make last second alterations in voting policies that could suppress certain voters. As a general rule, the directives are public record and usually posted on the state election official's website.

Recommendation #2: Election Observers

In many states there is a statute that allows the placement of campaign or political party election observers inside polling places and the county Boards of Elections on and around Election Day. Election observers generally have the right to be inside the polling place, look at the poll books, and talk to the poll workers and precinct judges. Usually they may observe the vote counting process as well. They can ask questions about policies and protocols, ask how many provisional votes happened and why, ask if there are any broken machines or other barriers to the voting process, or if any private technicians came in to fix any machines.

Election observers are not allowed to speak with voters while in the polling place or interfere with the voting process. Many election observers have used cellphones or tablets to take photos of problems, however may be restricted from taking any photos, particularly of anyone's ballot. Election observers may interview voters 100 feet away of the polling site.

The role of an election observer is to find and report problems: to the Election Protection headquarters to get help from attorneys or videographers; to the Board of Elections or Secretary of State's office; or to the media.

Recommendation #3: Obtain voter purge lists

In many states, there are a significant amount of voters who are de-registered in between elections. The lists of purged voters are public record, and can be obtained through a public records request from the Boards of Elections. After purged voters are identified, a campaign can be put together to re-register them.

Recommendation #4: Find out what equipment/companies and audit processes will be used

Obtain information from the state or each Board of Elections on: type of voting machines, poll books, tabulators, opti-scan equipment; who is responsible for equipment maintenance; and audit practices used in the state. The information may be found online through an internet search or through a public records request at the Boards of Elections or Secretary of State's office.

Election integrity activists have compiled information about most types of equipment which can be found on the internet. This information is important so that potential Election Day problems can be anticipated, quickly analyzed and brought to the attention of election officials or a court of law.

It is important to know exactly who will be performing technical support on Election Day, particularly if, at a polling site, someone not affiliated with the official tech support team shows up to "recalibrate" or otherwise tamper with the voting machines.

In some states the central tabulators at the Boards of Elections or Secretary of State's office lack audit logs. This needs to be discovered ahead of Election Day and activists must insist audit logs be put in place and made available so the results can be examined if there are irregularities.

Recommendation #5: Obtain voting machine allocation

Find out the location of polling places and the allocation of machines at each polling site, county by county. Many states, by statute or case law, set a standard for number of machines allocated per voter, e.g., Ohio is one machine per 100 voters. Again, this information is obtained through a request of the Boards of Elections. Some smaller rural counties may not have an allocation report. If it is determined there aren't enough machines for the number of voters, public pressure must be put on the Boards of Elections or a lawsuit could be threatened. There is federal case law supporting a reasonable number of voting machines per voter.

Recommendation #6: Know the state voter ID laws

It is important to know and communicate to voters precisely what ID's are required for voting in the state. Often, college students are targeted with ID laws.

Recommendation #7: Poll worker training

It is essential to obtain the state's poll worker training manuals and know the policies. In many cases, poll workers may be improperly trained, and a reference to the manual will correct the problem.

Recommendation #8: Watch absentee ballots and early voting sites for irregularities

In past elections, there have been problems because voters were not aware that mailing the absentee ballot required two stamps, and sometimes incorrect absentee ballots are sent out. Also, if there are early voting sites, it is important to make sure there are enough voting machines, that the hours the polls are open are well promoted, voters are aware of the locations, and the ballots have the correct information.

Recommendation #9: Paper ballots

Some states that use voting machines also allow voters to request a paper ballot on Election Day. It should be determined if the state will provide paper ballots at the polls and ensure that poll workers are trained in their use. Paper ballots are helpful as back-up in the event of machine breakdowns or long lines at the machines.

Recommendation #10: Tell voters to check their registration online

The cut-off date for voter registration is usually 30 days prior to Election Day. When campaigning, volunteers should encourage all voters to check the Board of Elections website, or go to the Board in person to verify that they are registered and confirm their voting location. Many people who have not moved and/or have voted in the same place for decades have found themselves removed from the voting rolls and/or have a changed voting location, and are forced to vote provisionally on Election Day.

Recommendation #11: Set up a Voter Hotline

The Election Protection campaign should create a phone number for voters to call when they have problems at the polls and promote it heavily before the election. If possible, it should connect to a number that can be answered by several people, and volunteers should staff the phones all day on Election Day. Often, calls addressing voter problems from the campaign directly to the Board of Elections officials can resolve the issues quickly. Also, election integrity activists/videographers/attorneys can be dispensed to the voter's location to investigate and solve problems, contact the media, obtain an affidavit, or protest as necessary.

Recommendation #12: Vigilance on provisional voting practices

It is important to become familiar with the state's practices on the use of provisional ballots: confirm what information is necessary for the voter to provide on the ballot and what is mandated to be written on the envelope. Provisional ballots have been discarded for lack of a zip code, or voters printing "below" rather than "on" the line. Some states allow voters who were forced to vote provisionally to go to the Board of Elections within 10 days after Election Day to provide identification/proof of address, which then may allow the vote to be counted.

Recommendation #13: Attorneys on standby

The Election Protection campaign needs attorneys in the field and on standby to file any necessary legal actions, injunctions or temporary restraining orders in response to violation of election laws on Election Day. The attorneys, paralegals and election protection activists should have documents and forms ready, such as self-executing federal affidavit forms and pre-drawn complaints that can be quickly filled in for each legal violation.

Recommendation #14: Videographers, tweeters, reporters

An easy way to immediately call attention to election irregularities is to encourage voters to record any unacceptable behavior or voting machine problems at the polls. Cellphone photos can be posted on a Facebook page, Twitter account, Instagram, and easily sent to the news media. The campaign should create an election protection website to post immediate reports about what's going on during Election Day, to give advice to voters, to warn voters of possible voting issues, and to report egregious voting irregularities.

Recommendation #15: Screenshots of election results

There have been various reports of people watching election results on TV or online during election night and seeing vote totals and percentages flipping. Election results should be monitored online throughout election night, particularly the results reported directly from the central tabulators at the Boards of Elections and the Secretary of State's office. Election protection activists can be assigned specific Board of Elections websites to watch, and to record screenshots of results every 15 minutes or half hour when the vote totals are updated. It is important to look out for times when the computers "go down" or the site goes offline, as that is a clue that the totals might come back "flipped."

PART ONE: "STRIP"

The foundation of election theft is the manipulation of race as a "divide and conquer" strategy. It began with the first Jim Crow, chattel slavery.

Slavery in various forms has existed since the dawn of time. But in the colonies of British North America, and then in the United States, it took on a uniquely virulent incarnation.

Chattel slavery was of course a horrific, brutal labor system, designed primarily in the American South to power a network of plantations that produced tobacco, cotton, indigo, rice and other hot weather crops that could be grown in large fields.

But it also had a larger purpose here. Our "peculiar institution" was meant to divide black laborers from white in a caste system that would guarantee they'd never unite in rebellion. As we'll see, this originated with the infamous Bacon's Rebellion of 1675 in Virginia, in which indentured servants of both races joined forces. Plantation owners vowed to make sure that never happened again.

When the United States became an independent country, plantation owners also vowed to secure political benefit from their slaves. Thus, they wrote into the Constitution a "3/5ths clause" that gave slave owners additional representation for their slaves, even though those slaves could not vote. That additional vote count guaranteed that every president from Jefferson to Lincoln either owned slaves or his vice president did. And that the Congress was strongly controlled by slave owners right up to the outbreak of Civil War.

After the Civil War, with formal slavery abolished, a "Jim Crow" system of racial segregation overtook the South. Enforced by the Democratic Party and its Ku Klux Klan terror wing, white landowners updated the realities of slavery to again keep blacks and whites apart. The root of racism since 1865 has been the treatment of legally freed African-Americans as something less than human, guaranteeing all whites a sense of superiority and an economic leg up. When the Populist and Socialist movements that campaigned most powerfully from the 1880s to 1920s worked to overcome this separation, they were hammered by the court and electoral systems through a series of stolen elections and twisted, race-based legal decisions, and the fusion of the Democratic and Republican Parties in the 1917 municipal races in the Northeast.

Confirmed by the Supreme Court in the 1890s, this updated Jim Crow caste system again guaranteed that blacks in the South (and parts of the North) would not be allowed to vote, and that they would be carefully divided from whites by caste as well as class.

Since 1970 the primary weapon for suppressing the minority vote has been the third Jim Crow, the Drug War. In the tradition of Bacon's Rebellion and the Populist/Socialist upheavals, blacks and whites once again began to unite during the Civil Rights and anti-war movements of the 1950s and 1960s.

In response, Richard Nixon's Republican Party invoked the divide-and-conquer "War on Drugs." Confronted with the liberalization of the southern Democratic Party, Nixon feared that black votes might remake America's political map.

In GOP eyes there was only one solution: disenfranchise the African-American population, along with young and Latino voters who were leaning strongly to the left.

In 1972 Nixon pointedly ignored a powerful report from his own Blue Ribbon Shafer Commission on drug use and escalated the attack on marijuana and other drugs. In the 45 years since, a staggering 41 million Americans have been arrested for pot and other controlled substances. That's a number of human beings that exceeds the populations of more than 150 other countries worldwide. It has left the United States with the largest prison population in the history of the modern world (while having little or no impact on the actual use of drugs).

As Michelle Alexander has shown in her landmark book *The New Jim Crow*, the majority of those incarcerated have been black and Latino, with a devastating impact on our elections. Millions of these mostly young, mostly male citizens have been stripped of their right to vote, as well as their ability to maintain families, obtain work and meaningfully participate in the political lives of their communities.

All this has been by design. Once again, a new Jim Crow policy has been delegated by a ruling elite to strip our non-white population of its ability to exercise its fair share of power in our electoral process, and to unite with whites in political action.

In the 1890s, rising industrial interests committed the nation to a fourth Jim Crow, a course of race-based global empire. The US already had a history of foreign intervention, dating to Thomas Jefferson's 1803 use of our fledgling navy to fight pirates along the coast (the "shores of Tripoli") of what's now Libya. That was followed by the conquest of the North American continent, with genocidal warfare used against the indigenous peoples who'd lived here 10,000 years.

By the 1890s, with the frontier consumed, America's giant corporations began to expand overseas. They started with Hawaii (a constitutional monarchy) and then pushed into Cuba, Puerto Rico, Guam, the Philippines and beyond. In all cases these interventions involved the white-ruled US interfering with the political systems of non-white nations.

In discussing this fourth Jim Crow we include an extensive (though not complete) list of these interventions. It underscores the reality that our own political system has become an imperial juggernaut, with the inevitable blowback bound to obliterate any residual pretense to real democracy at home.

Generally there's been an attempt to portray these interventions as benign, meant to bring democracy, progress and the Christian faith to Third World nations. In fact, they've been largely economic in purpose – a "Dollar Diplomacy" meant to grab for our major corporations new frontiers for cheap resources, exploited labor and expanded markets.

Their impact on our own political system has been catastrophic. They've established the US as a corporate-ruled race-based empire, fueling the growth of a military whose intrinsic power overshadows our entire electoral process.

And they've given our intelligence operations, most importantly from the Central Intelligence Agency (CIA), a long history of overturning elections and stripping mostly non-white nations of their right to self-rule. At the US Senate's landmark Church hearings in the 1970s, the Agency admitted to at least 5,000 such interventions in just the quarter-century since the end of World War II.

This entrenched tradition of contempt for the democratic process overseas came home electronically in 1988, when former CIA chief George Herbert Walker Bush won a statistically impossible New Hampshire primary victory over Bob Dole on newly installed electronic voting machines.

Overall, with more than 900 military bases, and troops or military advisors in 175 countries worldwide, the militarization of our own political processes has become entrenched. Perfected covert and overt techniques of stripping our non-white constituencies of their rights has become an integral part of all American elections.

All that has set the stage for the fourth and fifth Jim Crows – the electronic flipping of our elections.

In the meantime, each of these five original Jim Crows has devastated America's ability to evolve and thrive. The more we can know about them, the better able we will be to fight and defeat them. They have stripped our ability to function as an integrated, advanced body of human beings. They need, once and for all, to be buried.

THE FIRST JIM CROW:
Slavery and the 3/5ths Clause

For 400 years, race and slavery have divided and conquered us.

In 1619, Africans first came to Jamestown as indentured servants. Working conditions were harsh, but their basic human rights were assumed. Most achieved freedom. At least one eventually employed other workers.

As historian Lerone Benette, Jr., has put it:

> Before Jim Crow, before the invention of the Negro or the white man or the words and concepts to describe them, the Colonial population consisted largely of a great mass of white and black bondsmen, who occupied roughly the same economic category and were treated with equal contempt by the lords of the plantations and legislatures. Curiously unconcerned about their color, these people worked together and relaxed together.

But after black and white indentured servants united in the 1675 Bacon's Rebellion, Virginia landowners invented America's "peculiar institution" to separate the races.

Essentially a "bribe" to the whites, American chattel slavery cast blacks into an abyss of sub-human barbarity. They (and their children) became slaves for life. White "owners" could sell, torture, rape and murder their black "property" with no legal penalties.

With that came Slave Codes meant to completely degrade African immigrants and their progeny. They gave whites a higher status that would permanently divide them. No longer would whites and blacks work, play or join in rebellion together.

Poor whites could now tower (and cower) over a "slave caste." The Jim Crow abyss still gives them the illusion of "superiority" to which many cling with fear and desperation. Those who wonder at the longevity of racism must always remember that this is what gives even the most destitute and desperate white person a sense of being better than at least someone else on this Earth.

In 1787, as slavery persisted, the wealthy white men who drafted the US Constitution were primarily bankers, merchants, lawyers, military men, large farm operators and slave owners.

The public forced them to concede a Bill of Rights. But voting rights and procedures were largely left to the states.

The southerners got an Electoral College that included a "3/5ths clause." Slaves (who could not vote themselves) were counted for 3/5ths of a vote for president and in establishing Congressional districts.

Thus all presidents from Washington to Lincoln either owned slaves or their vice presidents did, and the South dominated the House of Representatives.

It all began with the Slave Codes:

- Enslaved African-Americans were stripped of all human rights. "Owners" and other whites were free to sell, rape, torture and kill black Americans without legal penalties.

- In many colonies and then states, it became illegal for free whites to fraternize with enslaved African-Americans.

- Racial intermarriage was illegal in many states until the 1960s.

- Slaves could not speak to whites without permission.

- Slaves could not testify in court except against other slaves.

- Slaves could not own property.

- Slaves could not earn their own wages, or buy or sell anything.

- Three slaves could not gather together without white supervision.

- Slaves could not travel outside plantations without a pass from their owners.

- Slaves could not marry and had no rights pertaining to their children.

- It was a capital crime to teach a slave to read, or for one to read even the Bible.

- "The Great Fear" ruling class whites embedded in the Slave Codes still divides black from white, permeates American life, and corrupts our electoral process.

- Both the British and the Americans offered blacks their freedom in exchange for joining their respective armies.

- During the Revolution, many blacks fought alongside whites on both sides.

- After the Revolution, African-Americans in many northern states could vote if they owned enough property to qualify.

    (Only Quaker-dominated New Jersey gave women the right to vote, which was rescinded in 1808).

- By most accounts when the US was governed by the Articles of Confederation, the majority of US citizens opposed the proposed new Constitution, which was drafted in secret in Philadelphia in the summer of 1787. The drafters were an elite group of bankers, lawyers, merchants, politicians, military leaders, plantation owners, and the printer/publisher Ben Franklin. There were no small farmers, workers, sailors, women, African-Americans, Indians or other "ordinary citizens" in the deliberations, which were held behind locked and guarded doors. The Convention sought ratification from nine of the twelve states (Vermont had not yet joined the union). Many believed the process would fail. By the time it came for New York to vote, nine states had ratified. But New York's approval was still critical. A strong majority of the convention was opposed, then somehow shifted to a 30-27 vote for ratification, which was essential to the Constitution's success. Had all electors voted as they were instructed by the populace, New York's ratification convention would have failed. At least some of those who switched their votes to negate the wishes of their constituents apparently received substantial material rewards later on.

- In 1800, the 3/5ths clause allowed Thomas Jefferson to win 74-65 in an Electoral College that otherwise would have gone 65-62 for John Adams. Jefferson owned (and fathered) some of the slaves that counted toward his victory.

- In 1800, 1824, 1876, 1888 and 2000, the candidate who came in second in the official popular vote has won the Electoral College.

- Until 1860 many states used property qualifications to exclude both whites and blacks from voting.

- When Elbridge Gerry rigged representational districts to favor his party in the 1790s, critics said they looked like salamanders; "gerrymandering" creates a situation where politicians choose their voters, instead of voters choosing their preferred candidate, resulting in extremists from both sides holding safe congressional seats, and resulting in severe gridlock. Gerrymandering has disenfranchised poor voters (both black and white) ever since.

THE SECOND JIM CROW:
American Apartheid

Some 200,000 black soldiers (60,000 of whom died) empowered the Union victory over the Confederacy. By contrast, some 200,000 poor white draftees deserted the Confederate army, running from what they called "a rich man's war and a poor man's fight."

In 1869 President U.S. Grant sent federal troops into the South to guarantee black rights. This "Radical Reconstruction" joined freed African-Americans with poor whites in bi-racial governments, terrifying former slave owners.

The 1870 ratification of the 15th Amendment gave freed black men the right to vote. Many southern states were 40-50% black. With just a few white votes, the party of Lincoln could control much of the former Confederacy.

Under Grant, newly elected former slaves and poor white southerners established some of the world's first bi-racial governments and began a "Second American Revolution."

But the Democratic Party built by Andrew Jackson enfranchising white male voters, functioned as the "Party of Race and Slavery," and after the Civil War became the Party of apartheid.

- Beginning in 1865, the Ku Klux Klan served as the terror wing of the Democratic Party (in the 1970s it shifted its services to Richard Nixon's GOP).

- The election of 1876, in which stolen electoral votes elected Rutherford B. Hayes, brought the end of Reconstruction and stripped away federal protection of freed former slaves.

- From 1865 through the 1980s, more than 4,000 lynchings (more than 300 per year) terrorized the black community throughout the South, stripping its ability to organize or function as an effective political entity.

- The former Confederacy has since maintained a system of virtual slavery imposed on blacks wrongly imprisoned and then worked for years in hard unpaid contract labor.

- These former slaves and their progeny have been systematically stripped of their right to vote for 150 years.

- Until the 1964 ratification of the 24th Amendment the poll tax was used to strip southern blacks of the right to vote.

- So-called "literacy tests" with impossible demands were used extensively to strip southern blacks of the right to vote.

- Whites were exempted from these requirements through the "Grandfather clause" granting the right to vote to all (i.e., whites) whose grandfathers could vote.

- After Reconstruction, a Jim Crow system of apartheid separation carried on the tradition of separating blacks and whites.

- Republican Benjamin Harrison lost the popular vote to incumbent President Grover Cleveland in 1888, but won the presidency in the Electoral College exposing a system where the loser of the popular vote can win by receiving the electoral votes from a few key battleground states.

- In the 1886 Santa Rosa railroad case, a clerk enshrined corporations with the right to "personhood" even though Supreme Court's actual decision made no mention of it. This recording error ultimately led to the disastrous Citizens United decision in 2010.

- The 1890s Populist movement briefly united black and poor white southerners in a coalition shattered by the 1896 national election, followed by violent assaults that crushed progressive bi-racial governments in Wilmington, North Carolina (where 500 armed whites killed at least 14 citizens). Similar violent incidents occurred in other southern towns.

- Fueled by at least $15 million from robber baron corporations, the critical election of 1896 was stolen through intimidation, disenfranchisement and fraudulent vote counts engineered by Cleveland industrialist Mark Hanna, the Karl Rove of the day.

- The Supreme Court's 1896 *Plessy v. Ferguson* decision (the vote was 8-1) enshrined Jim Crow "separate but equal" segregation, stripping the ability of African-American and mixed race citizens to fully participate in national life.

- The Supreme Court's unanimous 1898 *Williams v. Mississippi* decision upheld the ability of states to strip blacks of their right to vote through the literacy test and poll tax, while upholding the grandfather clause that allowed whites to vote if their grandfathers had voted. The decision allowed the hanging of a black man convicted of murder by an all-white Mississippi jury.

- After large corporate donations fueled Theodore Roosevelt's victorious 1904 presidential campaign, he supported the 1907 Tillman Act limiting corporate donations to political campaigns.

- Official vote counts vastly understated support for Socialist labor leader Eugene V. Debs, who opposed Jim Crow segregation. The hugely popular Debs ran for president in 1900, 1904, 1908, 1912 and 1920, always drawing enormous crowds but somehow never exceeding a million officially counted votes. In 1916 he ran for Congress from his home town of Terre Haute, Indiana, but was stripped of all official support when his vote count was recorded as zero.

- Virginia-born Democrat Woodrow Wilson, an outspoken admirer of the Ku Klux Klan and Jim Crow apartheid, re-segregated much of the federal government by stripping thousands of African-Americans of their jobs.

- Not until 1937 did a black musician, pianist Teddy Wilson, perform in public with white musicians, in this case Jewish clarinetist Benny Goodman ("the King of Swing") and the Italian- American drummer Gene Krupa (who was later imprisoned for possessing marijuana).

- The American Revolution was won by a bi-racial army, but blacks were stripped of the right to serve in integrated units until 1947 (the same year Jackie Robinson integrated Major League Baseball).

- In 1947, segregation in the military and Major League Baseball were legally ended. Black veterans returning from World War II were far less willing to endure racial segregation than any previous generation.

- The unanimous 1954 Supreme Court *Brown vs. Board of Education* decision opened the legal door for an all-out war against Jim Crow. Throughout the late 1950s the Civil Rights Movement moved effectively to enhance the power of the African-American community, aiming especially to spread the right to vote.

- Beginning with Rosa Parks on December 1, 1955, the Montgomery bus boycott demonstrated the power of an organized activist community to defeat Jim Crow laws and customs.

- With lunch counter sit-ins, freedom rides and more, the spread of black activism (often spurred by returning black war veterans) began to re-shape the South.

- During the 1960 presidential election, the family of Martin Luther King asked the Nixon campaign to help get him out of jail, where he was being held for a non-violent protest. Nixon declined.

- But on the urging of his campaign manager and brother, candidate John Kennedy worked to get King released. The gesture represented a shift in the Democratic Party from its historical bedrock in southern racism to one of tolerance and political alliance with the black community.

- Established in 1828, Andrew Jackson's Democratic Party was the party of race and slavery until the 1930s, when some northern blacks were attracted to the party by Franklin Roosevelt's social programs. The black community made a major shift in 1936, when FDR ran for re-election, from the GOP to the Democrats. JFK's 1960 reach-out to Dr. King came with an implied commitment to civil rights and liberties. But blacks in the South were still essentially stripped of their right to vote.

- Dr. King's 1963 March for Jobs and Freedom in Washington DC attracted a crowd of 250,000 to the Lincoln Memorial, including about 60,000 whites. Less than three months later, JFK was assassinated.

- In 1964, the returning vision of a black-white alliance took shape during Mississippi Freedom Summer, when thousands of white college students poured into the South to work for voter rights. Tragically, Michael Goodman, James Cheney and Andrew Schwerner were murdered. Cheney was black; Goodman and Schwerner were both white. So was Viola Liuzzo, a Detroit housewife working for civil rights who was shot dead by Klansmen in a car that also carried an FBI agent.

- In the wake of JFK's murder, Lyndon Johnson pushed a powerful pro-integration agenda, including a Civil Rights Act, a Voting Rights Act and the 24th Amendment, banning the poll tax. He publicly worried that the Democrats may now have "lost the South." But blacks comprised 40% or more of many southern states, meaning if they were able to vote along with a relatively small percentage of liberal whites they could carry the South for a newly progressive Democratic Party.

- In 1968 Republican strategists launched their "Southern Strategy" aiming to switch southern whites from the Democrats to the GOP while trying to avoid appearing overtly racist. As Republican strategist Lee Atwater put it:
  You start out in 1954 by saying, "Nigger, nigger, nigger." By 1968 you can't say "nigger"—that hurts you. Backfires. So you say stuff like forced busing, states' rights and all that stuff. You're getting so abstract now [that] you're talking about cutting taxes, and all these things you're talking about are totally economic things and a byproduct of them is [that] blacks get hurt worse than whites. And subconsciously maybe that is part of it. I'm not saying that. But I'm saying that if it is getting that abstract, and that coded, that we are doing away with the racial problem one way or the other. You follow me—because obviously sitting around saying, "We want to cut this," is much more abstract than even the busing thing, and a hell of a lot more abstract than "Nigger, nigger."

- In 1968 Alabama Governor George Wallace staged an independent run for the White House. Before he was shot and forced into a wheelchair, Wallace demonstrated the power of the race card to attract working class white voters throughout the South and in some northern blue-collar areas. In 1972 on the eve of his victory in Michigan primary, Wallace was shot and paralyzed, ending his presidential run.

- But the GOP Southern Strategy couldn't carry the South with white votes alone. Many states of the former Confederacy were 40% or more black. If allowed to vote, black Democrats could win political control with just a small percentage of liberal white voters.

- The Civil Rights Movement succeeded in raising black voter participation. African-American registration rates soared in Georgia from 19.3% to 60.4%; in Alabama from 19.3% to 61.3%; in Mississippi from 6.7% to 66.5%; in Louisiana from 31.6% to 60.8%. With African-Americans now voting heavily for the Democrats, the Republicans will need to disenfranchise them if they're to take the South.

- After narrowly winning the White House in 1968, Nixon continued the war in Vietnam and courted a "Silent Majority" essentially portrayed as angry reactionaries. He attacked the hippie counter-culture and signaled his willingness to welcome southern white racists into the Republican Party. But the Drug War would be his ultimate assault weapon.

- In a Florida 2000 election officially decided by less than 600 votes, Republican Governor Jeb Bush and Florida Secretary of State Katherine Harris used rigged computer lists and an old Jim Crow law to disenfranchise more than 90,000 African-Americans and Latinos on the false pretense that they were former felons and thus could not vote. As primarily reported by investigator Greg Palast, the list was supplied by Choicepoint, a company that worked for the FBI and the US Justice Department. Katherine Harris, who was entrusted by the citizens of Florida to run a fair non-partisan election, was Co-Chair of the Bush-Cheney Election Committee in Florida while she ran the voting and the vote count.

- Jim Crow segregation stripped effective black participation in most southern elections through the entire 20th century, preventing passage of numerous proposed anti-lynching laws, finally prompting a Congressional apology in 2005, still without a formal anti-lynching law having been entered into the books.

- Millions of Americans, mostly black and Latino, are now being disenfranchised through apartheid-based photo ID requirements that mirror the old Jim Crow poll taxes.

THE THIRD JIM CROW:
The Drug War

The Nixon campaign in 1968, and the Nixon White House after that, had two enemies: the antiwar left and black people. You understand what I'm saying? We knew we couldn't make it illegal to be either against the war or black, but by getting the public to associate the hippies with marijuana and blacks with heroin, and then criminalizing both heavily, we could disrupt those communities. We could arrest their leaders, raid their homes, break up their meetings, and vilify them night after night on the evening news. Did we know we were lying about the drugs? Of course we did.
        John Ehrlichman, Nixon's domestic policy advisor

The Drug War's primary impact on our society has been to create the fundamental reality of a police state – to prevent young, African-American and Latino citizens from voting via racial profiling by law enforcement, mass incarceration and systematic disenfranchisement. The Drug War continues to lynch the political and cultural well-being of communities of color and to establish a multi-billion-dollar for-profit prison industry in which incarcerated Americans serve essentially as cash flow, regardless of the impact of their imprisonment on society as a whole.

It has also helped repress the possibility of another black/white alliance like those that arose with Bacon's Rebellion in 1675 and the more recent abolitionist, Populist/Socialist and Civil Rights movements.

By making illegal something so widely practiced as drug use, the Drug War has allowed the government to establish a de facto police state, in which virtually anyone can be arrested at any time. The particular focus on the black community has composed an organized assault not unlike what the US has been doing to Third World countries around the world.

So for the African-American community, since 1970, the Drug Enforcement Agency and its allied police forces have become the modern equivalent of the Ku Klux Klan.

Mass arrests and prison time are the legal lynchings used to neutralize young men of color. Today about one-third of all African-American men have been to prison and are thus disenfranchised.

The Drug War's companion mandate has been to provide a constant supply of new prisoners to sustain America's multi-billion-dollar corporate prison-industrial complex. To do that, it has provided more than 41,000,000 drug arrests from 1970 to 2015 – about 1,000,000 per a year. Around 60% of those arrested have been black or Latino. They have served as the cash flow for the modern prison-industrial complex.

Overall the Drug War is widely estimated to have cost American taxpayers more than $1,000,000,000,000. It would have been cheaper to send every arrestee to college.

Instead the Drug War has negated the rights of more than 20,000,000 black and Latino citizens since 1971, and has drained America's communities of color of immeasurable wealth and self-sufficiency.

The net effect has been to repress the political power of the African-American and Latino communities, and to render them even more vulnerable to the stripping of poll books and the power of electronic voting machines to flip elections:

At the core of the counter-culture was marijuana. Its cousin, industrial hemp, was grown by Thomas Jefferson and George Washington, and used for paper by Benjamin Franklin. Behind tobacco, hemp was the second-largest cash crop in early America. During World War II, the military commandeered much of Kansas to grow it for rope and other products critical to the war effort. Hemp has no psychotropic qualities and was never banned by any nation. Because of its similar appearance to marijuana, the growing of hemp was restricted by federal law, even though the military grew a whole state of it during

World War II.

Cannabis for smoking has been illegal under federal law since 1935. Its prohibition was pushed primarily by Harry J. Anslinger, who formerly worked to enforce the prohibition of alcohol. By the early 1970s, more than half the nation's high school and college students had tried it. About 10% used marijuana somewhat regularly.

Marijuana's public health impacts have long been a subject for debate. In the late 1960s, Harvard Medical Professor Lester Grinspoon set out to warn the young generation of marijuana's alleged health dangers. But his research made him reverse his opinion. Grinspoon soon endorsed marijuana's beneficial medical powers and became an outspoken advocate. His *Marihuana Revisited* essentially said that putting people in prison for possession of pot had far more negative health impacts than smoking it.

In part as a response to Grinspoon's findings, the movement to legalize cannabis and other controlled substances escalated throughout the late 1960s, with widespread expectations of an early end to prohibition. In 1970 the National Organization for Reform of Marijuana Laws (NORML) was founded.

Making such a widely used substance illegal had the effect of introducing a police state, where a substantial percentage of the population is always at risk of arrest and incarceration. The negative impacts on public life have been enormous. As a result of their arrests, millions of young citizens have been stripped of the ability to find jobs and to vote.

- In 1969, the Nixon Administration "warmed up" the roll-out of the Drug War with Operation Intercept, as its Customs Department stopped every vehicle crossing the Mexican border. Massive traffic jams lasted for days.

- On June 17, 1971, Nixon proclaimed drug use to be "public enemy number one." In a nation wracked by war, poverty, racial tensions and environmental degradation, it seemed an odd choice, until political calculations were taken into account.

- On March 22, 1972, the "National Commission on Marihuana and Drug Abuse" reported that "Looking only at the effects on the individual, THERE IS little proven danger of physical or psychological harm from the experimental or intermittent use of the natural preparations of cannabis." It called for "a social control policy seeking to discourage marijuana use" without prosecution. Nixon ignored the report and proceed to put marijuana prohibition on a military footing.

- According to some specialists in the drug rehabilitation field, Nixon's early programs did contain significant elements of meaningful treatment and health care. But they gradually diminished in the shadow of a massive, heavily armed assault on ubiquitous substances with a special focus on mass incarceration.

- The impacts have been devastating. As Michelle Alexander shows in her monumental *The New Jim Crow* (much of the research in this section stems from Professor Alexander's book), overall the US prison population in 1970 was around 300,000; in 2000 it was more than 2,000,000. As we write this in 2016, it is 2,200,000, more than seven times what it was in 1970.

- By our estimates, between 1970 and 2015, more than 41,000,000 Americans have been arrested in the Drug War, nearly a million every year. About half are for simple possession of marijuana. About 60% of those arrested are black or Latino.

- The 41,000,000 Drug War arrests exceed the entire populations of more than 150 of the countries in the world today.

- In July, 1973, Nixon created the Drug Enforcement Administration (DEA) consolidating a number of federal agencies with local task forces to escalate the arrest levels at the street level.

- As conceived by Nixon and GOP strategists, the Drug War became what Alexander describes as "a stunningly comprehensive and well-disguised system of racialized social control that functions in a manner strikingly similar to Jim Crow." Its aim, she says, is to disrupt and disenfranchise the African-American community, "decimating networks of mutual support and intensifying the shame and self-hate experienced by the current pariah caste."

- In essence, the Drug War represented within the US an assault on the black community running in tandem with armed "global Jim Crow" interventions and electoral manipulations in foreign, mostly non-white nations.

- As of 2016, some 500,000 Americans are behind bars for drug offenses, as opposed to an estimated 41,000 in 1980, says Alexander.

- According to Prof. Bruce Western of Princeton University, in 1980, 143,000 American black men were in prison, as opposed to 463,700 in college; in 2000 there were 791,600 black men in prison, as opposed to 603,032 in college.

- In 1983 Ronald and Nancy Reagan announced a new escalation of the Drug War. Ms. Reagan advised young people to "Just Say No." But, the Reagan administration took profits from the illegal sale of arms to Iran and illegally shifted them to Nicaragua's cocaine-dealing Contras. They poured much of that cocaine into US cities like Los Angeles and Miami, where it was turned into crack, decimating the black and Hispanic communities.

- In turn, the escalated Reagan Drug War imposed prison sentences far harsher on crack cocaine, used primarily in the black and Hispanic communities, than on equal quantities of powdered cocaine, used primarily in the white communities. Huge sentencing disparities have heightened the Drug War's disproportionate political impact on communities of color.

- From 1985 to 2000, drug offenses alone accounted for two-thirds of the rise in the American prison population, says Alexander.

- From 1960 to 1990, official crime rates in Finland, Germany and the US were nearly the same. But the US rate of incarceration quadrupled. In Finland it dropped 60% while remaining stable in Germany.

- Due largely to the Drug War, and defined largely by race, the US penal system has become the largest in the history of the world, both by numbers of inmates and by percentage of the general public incarcerated.

- With the rise of the Drug War and the Nixon/Reagan/Bush/Bush packing of the US Supreme Court with corporatist judges hostile to civil rights and liberties, the justice system has been decimated by the rapid erosion of the Bill of Rights. Actual adherence to the Fourth, Fifth, Sixth and Eighth Amendments has been vastly compromised.

- Though African-Americans use drugs in about the same proportion as whites, the incarceration rate for drug-related crimes among blacks is 20 to 50 times higher than for whites in some states.

- As a result of the Drug War, as much as 80% of young black males nationwide have criminal records, in many cases eliminating their ability to vote, find good jobs, sustain a family or participate in the political life of their communities.

- As of 2016, roughly one in every three young African-American men is under control of the criminal justice system, i.e. in prison, in jail, or on probation or parole. Millions have lost their right to vote, skewing the electorate strongly toward the GOP.

- *Huffington Post* reports that isolating for race as a factor, young black male incarceration in the US is ten times higher than it was in South Africa under apartheid.

- High-profile drug busts sometimes take on the surreal dimension of an open, all-out war on the black community. In 1999, for example, a drug bust in Tulia, Texas, jailed almost 15% of the entire town's black population. The charges were cooked up with uncorroborated false testimony of an individual informant who had been hired by the sheriff.

- Beyond its function in disenfranchising the black population, the Drug War has spawned a hugely profitable private prison system with a multi-billion-dollar stake in convicting as many bodies as possible to fill prison beds (or cots), insuring cash flow. Judges, lawyers, prison guards, prison construction and service businesses and other related enterprises share in the bonanza.

- The Drug War's financial incentives have been extended to local police departments with the 1978 Comprehensive Drug Abuse Prevention Act, allowing law enforcement to confiscate cash and "other things of value" related to alleged drug violations even in the absence of evidence, warrants or formal charges. Thus, police departments are enriched without accountability. Victims are often informed they can sue to get their property back, but that legal fees will likely exceed the value of what's been taken. Billions of dollars have been transferred from innocent private citizens into police department coffers through this nationwide scam, with virtually no accountability.

- From 1980 to 1984 massive increases in drug law enforcement money flowed into the FBI, DOD and DEA. Funding for drug use prevention, education and treatment was slashed.

- The 1988 Anti-Drug Abuse Act authorized public officials to deny student loans and enforce evictions from public housing against anyone convicted of a drug crime. The primary targets were African-American, who were again stripped of the right to vote.

- The Anti-Drug Abuse Act also expanded the use of the death penalty and required five-year minimum sentences for drug offenses, ensuring the destruction of innumerable lives, white and black.

- In 1990 the Ku Klux Klan officially announced its embrace of the Drug War, promising to "join the battle against illegal drugs" and become the "eyes and ears of the police," ensuring continuity with the Klan's historic function in denying blacks their right to vote.

- As a "new corporate Democrat," Arkansas Governor Bill Clinton revived the racist roots of the Party of Jackson and vowed to "never to be out-done" as a crime-fighter.

- When President Clinton escalated the Drug War, he disenfranchised still more African-Americans and further weakened the civil rights community. Clinton's "triangulation" on drugs and race heralded the Democrats' hostile refusal to say or do anything about the electronic voting machines used to steal elections from them.

- In 1992, amidst his first campaign for president, Clinton rushed back to Arkansas to oversee the execution of a mentally impaired black man named Ricky Ray Rector. Rector was so unaware of his situation he asked prison guards to preserve the dessert from his last meal until after he would be killed. After the execution, Clinton bragged that "no one can say I'm soft on crime."

- In his 1994 State of the Union address, Clinton endorsed a "three strikes and you're out" policy imposing life sentences on citizens convicted of three crimes, no matter how minor. Thousands of lives were ruined for petty misdeeds, much to the dismay of many outspoken judges. Clinton pardoned none of the victims. Decades later, he expressed limited public regret.

- Clinton marked another Drug War escalation by signing a $30 billion crime bill in August, 1994, along with other massive increases in police funding.

- According to the Justice Policy Institute, Clinton's "tough on crime" policies caused "the largest increases in federal and state prison inmates of any president in American history." Massive disenfranchisement accompanied the assault, meaning corporate Clinton Democrats enhanced the Republican strategy of curbing black votes and helping the GOP take control of Congress.

- With the Personal Responsibility and Work Opportunity Reconciliation Act Clinton "ended welfare as we know it," gutting welfare and food stamp assistance for anyone convicted of a drug violation, including simple possession of small quantities of marijuana, which Clinton admits to having smoked himself (allegedly without inhaling).

- Clinton inaugurated a "one strike and you're out" policy allowing public housing authorities to evict tenants based on a single marijuana conviction that might even have involved friends and relatives rather than the evictees themselves, further crippling the African-American community.

- During the 2000 presidential election, as reported by Greg Palast, Florida Governor Jeb Bush and Florida Secretary of State Katherine Harris used Choicepoint, a computer service to strip more than 90,000 voters from the state's registration rolls in an election decided by less than 600 votes. Mostly black and Hispanic voters were stripped of their ballots for having allegedly committed felonies, presumably many of them offenses imposed by the prosecution of the Drug War.

- George W. Bush never directly admitted to or denied having used marijuana amidst wide-spread reports that he smoked pot with great frequency.

- Under George W. Bush and the 2002 Help America Vote Act, electronic poll books and voting machines spread throughout the US without opposition from Democrats, who also ignored the impact of the Drug War on electoral outcomes.

- In 2002, the ACLU reported that 1/3 of the nation's crack users were black, but 80% of those sentenced for it were black.

- In 2009, 4.7% of all black American males were incarcerated, as were

1.8% of Latinos and 0.7% of whites.

- In 2009, according to the Department of Justice, African-Americans made up 12% of the general US population but 60% of the prison population. Most inmates in the prison system are not allowed to vote.

- According to the American Civil Liberties Union (ACLU), blacks and whites still smoke marijuana in about the same ratio to population, but blacks are 3.73 times more likely to be arrested for marijuana use as whites, even though they comprise less than 20% of the general population.

- Barack Obama wrote explicitly about having used cocaine and marijuana, but as president did not de-escalate an anti-drug campaign that disenfranchised thousands of black citizens all through his time in office.

- Despite explicit promises, Obama's federal police continued to arrest users of medical marijuana in some 20 states where it has been made legal.

- In 2013, there were nearly 7,000,000 Americans in prison, local jails, on probation or parole.

- At 716 per 100,000 citizens, the US has the highest incarceration rate in the world. Russia locks up 455 per 100,000. Germany imprisons 76 per 100,000, Italy 85 per 100,000 and Sweden 60 per 100,000.

- According to the Center for Prison Studies, more black males are now incarcerated in the US than the combined total prison populations of Argentina, Canada, Germany, India, Japan, Finland, United Kingdom and Lebanon.

- With 4% of the world's population, the US now has 25% of its prison population.

- According to the ACLU, five times as many whites use drugs as blacks, but a black man is 10 times as likely to be arrested for using them.

- Blacks represent 12% of the total population of drug users (corresponding to the percentage of African-Americans in the US) but 38% of the people arrested for drugs are black, and 59% of those imprisoned for drugs are black.

- According to a 2009 report given to Congress by the Center for American Progress, 13% of American black men are currently denied the right to vote, a rate seven times the national average for all citizens.

- According to the Sentencing Project, 23% of African-Americans in Florida are denied the right to vote; 22% in Kentucky; 20% in Virginia.

- According to the Sentencing Project, 48 states (Maine and Vermont are the exceptions) prohibit voting while imprisoned for a felony; 35 states ban citizens on felony parole from voting; 31 states don't allow people on probation to vote; 4 states deny felons the right to vote even after completing sentences; 8 states have other restrictions. Some 2.6 million Americans have completed prison sentences but cannot vote.

- Amidst a rising tide of marijuana decriminalization, Colorado and Washington state made it legal in 2014. Oregon, Alaska and the District of Columbia have joined them. Yet, federal prosecutions continue.

- In the early 2010s, in part due to a state-by-state de-escalation of the Drug War, the US prison population has begun to drop.

Overall the Drug War has shifted America's balance of power in Congress and in many state and local governments from the Democrats with their large base in the African-American community to the Republicans. Gutting the political power of southern blacks has helped the GOP take both Houses of Congress and has vastly enhanced its nationwide power, thanks in large part to the continued prosecution of the Drug War by Democrats Clinton and Obama.

With more than 20,000,000 arrests of mostly young black men, the Drug War has gutted the African-American community as thoroughly as the Klan lynchings and Jim Crow apartheid that followed the Civil War.

Over 45 years the Drug War's mass imprisonment and communal vote denial have matched many US overseas interventions in their impact on targeted nations...in this case the African-American community. Overall the Drug War remains one of the most thoroughly anti-democratic events in all of US history.

The racist drug war mirrored an even more brutal assault on the developing world. For two centuries, the US has used its military to strip more nations of their democratic rights than any other. Those nations have been predominantly non-white.

PART TWO: "FLIP"

THE FOURTH JIM CROW:
Race-Based Election Theft Goes Global

In their final addresses, George Washington warned against entangling alliances, and Dwight Eisenhower against the military-industrial complex.

William Blum's book *Killing Hope: U.S. Military and C.I.A. Interventions since World War II* lists 57 instances of the United States overthrowing, or attempting to overthrow, a foreign government since the Second World War.

Our military and intelligence agencies have regularly interfered in elections, overthrown or killed the rightful victors and installed regimes friendly to the financial interests of American corporations.

The blowback has reshaped our own political system.

The art and science of subverting foreign governments has come home to roost.

General Smedley Butler, once America's top-ranking Marine, winner of two Congressional Medals of Honor, put it this way:

I served in all commissioned ranks from second lieutenant to Major General. And during that period I spent most of my time being a high-class muscle man for Big Business, for Wall Street and for the bankers. In short, I was a racketeer for capitalism. I suspected I was just part of the racket all the time. Now I am sure of it.

In 1933 General Butler was recruited by American corporate leaders to lead an army against the US government and to assassinate newly-elected President Franklin Roosevelt, but he refused, and confirmed the conspiracy in Congressional testimony. None of the corporate conspirators were sent to prison.

That "racket" has been perpetrated primarily against people of color. The US now maintains at least 900 bases in 175 countries throughout the world at a cost of hundreds of billions of dollars annually. Our practice is to allow smaller nations to elect their own leaders. If those leaders threaten American corporate interests, they are stripped of power (and often their lives) and their nations are called "rogue" or part of the "axis of evil." The locals are told to try again.

But the habit of trashing inconvenient governments can rebound. It can make people think such behavior is acceptable, even on our home shores. And it can make the agencies involved with pulling off those overthrows extremely effective at doing it at home:

- In 1804 Haitian slaves overthrew their French masters, but no US president would recognize the new nation until Abraham Lincoln did it in 1863. The US has since invaded Haiti and overthrown numerous elected governments there, stripping the nation of its democratic rights while propping up heinous dictators like "Papa Doc" Duvalier and his son "Baby Doc."

- In 1805, Thomas Jefferson approved a treaty with "Barbary Coast" rulers who'd been pirating American shipping. Skirmishes with what are now Libya, Tunisia and Algeria (along the "shores of Tripoli") were America's first on behalf of corporate commerce.

- In 1824, Secretary of State John Quincy Adams drafted the "Monroe Doctrine" proclaiming US hegemony over the entire western hemisphere.

- In 1832, Andrew Jackson sent a military expedition to Sumatra, a large Indonesian island, in retaliation for native attacks on an American ship involved in the pepper trade, killing as many as a thousand unarmed civilians. A later second expedition repeated much of the carnage in 1839.

- In the 1830s, American settlers re-introduced slavery to Texas, where Mexico had abolished it in 1821. In 1836 Texas became a slave republic. It became a slave state in 1845. It joined the Confederacy in 1861. Today its prison system incarcerates more than 170,000 citizens, a majority of them black or Latino, and at various times (as under former Governor George W. Bush) has executed more than any other state.

- Texas statehood led to the 1846-48 US invasion of Mexico and its capital (the "Halls of Montezuma") by President James K. Polk. Annexation soon followed of much of what is now New Mexico, Arizona, California, Nevada, Colorado, Utah, Wyoming and Oklahoma. Latinos returning to these lands are now often called "illegal immigrants."

- In 1854, Commodore Matthew Perry used "gunboat diplomacy" as our warships sailed into Edo (Tokyo) harbor to strip unwilling Japanese rulers of their ability to keep their archipelago closed to American commerce.

- In December 1890, US troops slaughtered more than 300 starving, freezing Lakota, ending resistance of duly constituted tribal peoples in the west at Wounded Knee. In a matter of minutes they stripped America's tribal peoples of their final major independent presence in the west.

- In 1893, American sugar and pineapple barons staged a "revolution" to strip Hawaii of its centuries-old constitutional monarchy. Grover Cleveland refused to annex the archipelago, but in 1898 William McKinley said God gave him the green light.

- In 1898, the battleship Maine blew up in Havana Harbor (286 sailors died) where it was anchored in alleged support of Cubans rebelling against the Spanish Empire. American media and government blamed Spain (the Navy later admitted the Maine blew up from the inside). A bloody war with thousands of casualties lasted until 1903, as the US stripped Cuba, Puerto Rico, Guam and the Philippines of their ability to self-govern. The US ruled the Philippines until 1947, then supported the brutal dictatorship of Ferdinand Marcos. Based on hands-on examinations by US divers, the US Navy has conceded that the Maine was not sunk by Spain. It most likely blew up due to mishandling of the coal-burning power plant aboard the ship. The entire Spanish-American War was thus based on a lie.

- In 1899-1900, several thousand US troops helped suppress China's Boxer Rebellion and maintain "spheres of influence" through which the US and other industrial powers stripped China of its independence and much of its resources.

- In 1915, Woodrow Wilson invaded Mexico, again sending troops into the capital city, stripping what he called "our little brown brothers" of their independence.

- In 1917, despite massive popular resistance, Wilson entered World War I to "make the world safe for democracy," killing some 116,000 Americans, while violating the Constitution to imprison thousands of citizens who spoke out against the slaughter. Scores of peace advocates were stripped of their rights to free speech and were incarcerated until long after the war ended. Wilson used the post-war Red Scare to illegally crush Debs's Socialist Party despite its constitutional status as a legitimate, long-standing political organization millions of Americans accepted as a viable alternative to corporate domination.

- The Lusitania sinking was a key "provocation" used by Woodrow Wilson as a pretext to declare war on Germany. US divers have since confirmed that the Lusitania was in fact carrying munitions to the British in defiance of international law. The ship sank extremely fast almost certainly because one or both of the torpedoes that hit it set off the explosives it was carrying illegally.

- In 1918, Wilson sent 7,000 US troops (70 died) to support White Russian Tsarist aristocrats in their war against revolutionary "Reds."

- In the 1920s the US invaded and overthrew the duly elected governments of numerous Latino nations in the corporate service of what Smedley Butler called a "Wall Street racket."

- From 1912-32, in a series of both overt and covert "Banana War" interventions, US troops may have killed as much as 10% of Nicaragua's entire population while stripping its independence.

- In El Salvador, as many as 40,000 people died in a 1932 grassroots uprising crushed by US troops.

- From 1933-45 Franklin Roosevelt's Good Neighbor Policy refrained from overthrowing Latin American governments, including an otherwise predictable invasion of Mexico as it nationalized its oil reserves into PEMEX (Petroleos Mexicanos) in 1938.

- From 1946-49 the US-backed Greek Army installed a fascist dictatorship to crush rebels who had fought the Nazis in World War II. At a critical moment, Stalin refused to support the Communist rebels, dooming them. Meanwhile, the Truman Doctrine claimed the US right to intervene anywhere and strip the independence of any country in which America's military claimed Communism might expand.

- A 1949 CIA-backed coup stripped Syria's civilian government of power and installed Housni el- Za'im, an army chief of staff who supported American oil interests.

- In 1952, the US supported the return of dictator Fulgencio Batista, who overthrew Cuba's democratically elected government.

- Working with the United Kingdom, the US in 1953 stripped Iran's duly elected Prime Minister Mohammad Mossadegh from power, installing the dictatorial Shah whose infamous CIA-supported Savak secret police begin a 25-year reign of torture and terror. The coup was coordinated by Kermit Roosevelt, Jr., grandson of Theodore Roosevelt.

- The CIA in 1954 overthrew the democratically elected government of Jacobo Arbenz and installed Castillo Armas, a military dictator, with some 250,000 Guatemalan disenfranchised peasants then dying in a 25-year civil war.

- In 1956, Dwight Eisenhower stopped elections (sanctioned by the United Nations) for Vietnamese unification, stripping from power Ho Chi Minh, who was expected to win with as much as 80% of the popular vote. Two decades of ensuing civil war and US intervention killed millions of Vietnamese and 58,000 Americans.

- In 1959, the US installed "Papa Doc" Duvalier, whose dictatorship, carried on by his son, stripped Haitians of all rights until 1986.

- In 1961, the CIA launched the Bay of Pigs invasion meant to overthrow Cuba's revolutionary regime, but incoming President John F. Kennedy withheld air support and an expected public uprising did not materialize. In response, Cuba asked the USSR to install missiles, prompting a global confrontation in 1962 that nearly brought on an atomic holocaust. The USSR removed the missiles after JFK promised not to invade Cuba and to remove US missiles from Turkey.

- In 1961, renegade elements linked to the CIA assassinated the democratically elected Congolese leader Patrice Lumumba, a former postal worker. By 1965 the US installed the brutal dictator Joseph Mobutu who, along with Western interests, stripped the country of billions of dollars which he deposited in overseas bank accounts.

- In 1961, the CIA may have helped assassinate Dominican dictator Rafael Trujillo, stripping the Republic of its democracy. In April, 1965, after years of turmoil, President Johnson sent in the 82nd Airborne to install the dictator Joaquin Balaguer.

- In 1961, CIA-led forces replaced Peru's popular elected President Juan Velasco Alvarado with Vice President Carlos Julio Arosemena Monroy, who was replaced two years later with a military junta after he somehow insulted the US ambassador.

- In 1963, the CIA stripped from power the duly elected Iraqi government of President Qasim, replacing it with the Ba'ath Party of dictator Saddam Hussein.

- In early November 1963, the CIA orchestrated the kidnapping and murder of South Vietnamese Prime Minister Ngo Dinh Diem and his brother, replacing the Prime Minister with a long line of pro-US dictators, many of them involved in the opium trade in Laos centered around Air America.

- On November 22, 1963, 20 days after Diem's murder, President John F. Kennedy was assassinated in what a majority of Americans believe was a conspiracy. In the wake of Kennedy's murder, efforts to end the Cold War, outreach to Cuba and the Soviet Union, and JFK'S determination to remove troops from Vietnam all came to a crashing halt. Our nation has never really recovered. The official "Warren Commission" that blamed the assassination on the Lee Harvey Oswald included Allen Dulles, former head of the CIA, whom JFK had fired after the Bay of Pigs fiasco.

- Brazil's democratically elected Joao Goulart government was overthrown in 1964, followed by a series of CIA-supported military dictatorships lasting on-and-off through much of the next two decades.

- A CIA-coordinated 1965 coup stripped Indonesian nationalist Sukarno from power, replacing him with the brutal kleptocrat Suharto, who looted the country. At least 800,000 people died in the slaughter, which the CIA called "a model operation."

- A CIA-led 1967 coup stripped from Greece its democratically elected Prime Minister Papandreou and flipped into power the dictatorial "rule of the colonels," lasting through 1974.

- On April 4, 1968, Dr. Martin Luther King, Nobel Prize-winning non-violent leader of the US Civil Rights movement, was murdered in Memphis. Accused assassin James Earl Ray denied killing him and King's family eventually agreed. King's murder crippled the grassroots movement aimed at ending Jim Crow segregation (see next section) and sparked nationwide rioting that killed scores of Americans. Millions of Americans still believe King was killed by a yet another arm of the US government, most likely the FBI.

- On June 5, 1968, Democratic presidential front-runner Robert F. Kennedy died in a shooting blamed on another lone gunman. Bobby was following his slain brother's commitments to end Jim Crow, bring peace to Vietnam and stop the Cold War. His death gave the nomination to Vice President Hubert Humphrey, who then narrowly lost to Richard Nixon under the darkest of circumstances. At least one RFK associate Paul Schrade, also shot that day, believes accused assassin Sirhan Sirhan was innocent, and that the shots that stripped Kennedy from us all were fired by someone still unknown. Robert F. Kennedy, Jr., has asked that Sirhan be released from prison and a new investigation be opened into his father's death.

- To win the 1968 election, Nixon illegally sabotaged US-Vietnam peace talks just days before the presidential balloting. In wiretapped phone conversations Nixon's liaison, Anna Chennault, illegally asked the South Vietnamese to nix a truce so Nixon could be elected president. "Hold on," she told South Vietnamese diplomat Bui Diem, "we are gonna win." Nixon then lied to President Lyndon Johnson when asked about it in the Oval Office. Johnson never made a public disclosure. The war dragged on another seven years with hundreds of thousands of Vietnamese and more than 20,000 Americans being killed beyond the 38,000 already dead. The treasonous Nixon/ Chennault intervention stripped the US public of an election outcome that might have ended the war earlier and saved thousands of lives.

- In 1970, Nixon's CIA overthrew Prince Sihanouk of Cambodia, which Nixon illegally bombed. When the bombing became public, protests erupted at scores of US campuses. On May 4, four unarmed students were shot dead at Kent State, Ohio, by National Guardsmen using live ammunition. Audio tapes indicate the Guard was verbally ordered to open fire. Two days later two more unarmed students were shot dead at Jackson State, Mississippi. Stripping Cambodia of its popular ruler led to a coup by Pol Pot, embraced by US Secretary of State Henry Kissinger. Pol Pot was a criminal psychopath who killed as many as 3,000,000 Cambodians.

- In 1973, Salvador Allende, Chile's duly elected socialist prime minister, was assassinated in a CIA-coordinated coup in 1973. Chile had been the western hemisphere's third-oldest republic, dating back to 1810. Having been stripped of its democracy by US intervention, the country was flipped to the brutal dictator Augusto Pinochet, who ruled with an iron fist and greedy hand for the next 17 years.

- On April 30, 1975, two decades of US intervention ended with a panicked retreat from the rooftop of the Saigon embassy, leaving thousands of American supporters stranded among victorious North Vietnamese and Viet Cong forces. The slaughter was the direct result of Eisenhower's 1956 sabotage of legitimate national elections.

- In 1975, duly elected Australian Labor Party Prime Minister Edward Whitlam was stripped of power when the CIA coerced the governor-general, a ceremonial imperial holdover appointed by the Queen, to install a more corporate-friendly regime. This overt operation was one of the few made public in which America intervened in the electoral affairs of a white-dominated country.

- In 1975, Congressional hearings held by Idaho Senator Frank Church and New York Representative Otis Pike, the CIA admitted to over 5,000 "benign operations" described as "election rigging" at the local, state and national level in foreign countries. Church lost re- election in a heavily funded right wing smear campaign. Pike declined to run again. The committee met stiff resistance against publishing its findings. The House refused to accept the Pike committee's report, but some of it was leaked to the *Village Voice* by TV news reporter Daniel Schorr. *The CIA and the Cult of Intelligence* by Victor Marchetti & John Marks, and Inside the Company by Philip Agee, about CIA covert operations, were both published in 1975. President Gerald Ford responded by appointing the Rockefeller "whitewashing committee" to minimize the damage from these published findings.

- In 1975, the CIA intervened in Angola's complex civil war involving Soviets and Cubans. Congress cut off funds in 1976, but the CIA sustained covert operations through the 1980s. Some 300,000 Angolans died in the course of the civil war.

- With the 1979 Soviet invasion of Afghanistan, the US began funding anti-communist Islamic fundamentalists including Osama bin Ladin's Al Quaeda, with which the US did not break until 1991. Bin Laden claimed "credit" for terror attacks on the World Trade Center in 1996 and 2001, among others.

- When leftist Sandinista rebels ousted Nicaragua's brutal CIA-sponsored dictator Somoza in 1979, his personal guard rebelled, transforming themselves in "Contras" who funded their opposition to the Sandinistas by shipping millions of dollars' worth of cocaine into the US, an operation also supported by the CIA. Much of that cocaine was converted into crack, which helped devastate and disenfranchise millions of Americans, many of them black and Latino.

- In November, 1979, Iranian students embittered by a quarter-century of US support for the Shah and his Savak torturers, took 55 American hostages in Teheran. Eight Americans died in a failed attempt to free them.

- In an apparent "October Surprise" operation, echoing Richard Nixon's 1968 interference with Vietnam peace talks, former CIA Director George H.W. Bush and later CIA Director William Casey were suspected of secretly persuading Iran's fundamentalist regime to hold US hostages through our presidential election to guarantee the victory of Ronald Reagan. The hostages were released in January, 1981, precisely as Reagan was sworn in as president.

- The US supported both sides in a ghastly 1980s war between Iran and Iraq, in which more than a million people died. Amidst the slaughter, US Secretary of Defense Donald Rumsfeld traveled to Baghdad to publicly embrace Iraqi dictator Saddam Hussein.

- In 1983, a suicide bomber blew up a US barracks in Beirut, killing 241 Americans, including 221 Marines and other military personnel. It was the US military's single deadliest day since Iwo Jima. Reagan pulled largely out of the Middle East, but two days later shifted public attention and attacked the tiny Caribbean island of Grenada, allegedly to protect US medical students there. While "rescuing" the students, Reagan brought in a new pro-US government.

- After US hostages returned from Tehran as he was being inaugurated, Reagan secretly sold arms to Iran at inflated prices. He claimed there was no connection between these illegal arms sales and the prolonged imprisonment of our hostages which guaranteed his election in 1980. Reagan then illegally slipped profits from these arms sales to cocaine-dealing Contras fighting to strip out Nicaragua's duly elected Sandinista government. In 1986, a CIA plane crashed with military supplies for the Contras which included a "Freedom Fighters Manual" outlining the use of political assassination, torture, interrogation techniques, extortion, bribery, blackmail, election rigging, economic sabotage and media manipulation. Amidst the massive Iran-Contra uproar, Reagan claimed no knowledge of the illegal money laundering scheme, but likened Contra coke pushers to America's Founding Fathers, and continued attempts to strip Nicaragua of its duly elected government.

- In 1986 the CIA tried to electronically rig elections for Philippine dictator Ferdinand Marcos. But mainframe computers broke down and technicians walked out, prompting international observers, including a US delegation led by Indiana Republican Senator Richard Lugar, to declare Corazon Aquino the winner. *The Power Game,* a documentary film by *New York Times* reporter Hedrick Smith, later called this the first documented CIA attempt to rig an election with computers.

- In 1987, the International Foundation for Election Systems (IFEF) promoted itself as the "world's premier election assistance organization." The IFEF was founded out of the Iran-Contra scandal with funds from the CIA-backed National Endowment for Democracy (NED). Documents from the scandal showed that in 1979, the IFEF received $125,000 from the NED to overthrow the

Sandinista government in Nicaragua, which happened in a 1990 election that installed Violetta Chamorro, a president friendlier to the US. In 2015, the IFEF web page listed more than 100 nations that it has worked with in supplying computer voting technology.

- In 1989, President George H.W. Bush, former head of the Central Intelligence Agency, sent the US military to arrest once-favored Panamanian dictator Manuel Noriega on drug charges. He was surrounded in a compound and "tortured" with constant loud rock music. Noriega surrendered and was brought to the US to stand trial. He attempted to expose US drug dealing in Panama, but was silenced by a federal judge and imprisoned. He remains imprisoned and his memoir *America's Prisoner: The Memoirs of Manuel Noriega* was published in 1997.

- In 1990, leftist priest Jean Bertrand-Aristide was elected Haiti's premier with 68% of the popular vote, but the CIA soon stripped his power with a military coup, using a global propaganda campaign to brand him as being "insane" for demanding higher wages for Haitian workers.

- George H.W. Bush's short-lived 1991 Operation Desert Storm forced Iraq's CIA-installed Saddam Hussein to leave the oil fields of Kuwait. A meeting with US diplomat April Glaspie was thought to have given Hussein the impression the US had no opinion on his deployment of troops in Kuwait. Despite few immediate casualties, more than 250,000 vets became eventually disabled by "Gulf War Syndrome," whose existence the US military initially denied. The Syndrome was attributed to vaccines and chemicals soldiers were exposed to and caused debilitating headaches, skin and respiratory disorders. At the time, Bush declined to strip Saddam of his power. Then-Secretary of State Madeleine Albright admitted that 500,000 or more innocent Iraqi children died as a result of infrastructure damage by bombs and the US sanctions against Iraq following the War.

- In 1993, Bill Clinton overthrew the Haitian dictatorship Bush had installed and helped re-install former president Aristide. But after his 2000 re-election, Aristide demanded France pay reparations for Haiti's original enslavement, so in 2004 US President George W. Bush supported Aristide being stripped from power yet again. Covert French and US operatives then flew him to the Central African Republican on a military plane. Aristide's wife later told

Congressional Representatives Charles Rangel and Maxine Waters that the US Ambassador threatened mass killings throughout Haiti if Aristide did not leave.

• In 1996, investigative reporter Gary Webb published an award-winning expose in the *San Jose Mercury News* demonstrating that the CIA was running crack cocaine into Los Angeles and beyond in cooperation with the Contras trying to overthrow the government of Nicaragua. Webb's widely acclaimed book *Dark Alliance* was savaged in the corporate media. Webb lost his job and marriage. He died in 2004 in an apparent suicide in which he allegedly shot himself in the head twice.

• On September 11, 2001, some 3,000 Americans died in attacks on the World Trade Center and Pentagon, with "credit" claimed by Al Quaeda, the fundamentalist Islamic terror organization founded with US support during the Afghan war. Coming just nine months after the disputed inauguration of George W. Bush, bitter controversy still rages over exactly how this happened and who is responsible.

• After the 9/11 attack, huge quantities of toxic dust poured into the New York region, impacting the health of millions with no significant warning or direction from the Bush administration. Thousands of courageous clean-up workers suffer impacts that echo Agent Orange abuse in Vietnam and Gulf War Syndrome.

• The 9/11 attacks were followed immediately by anthrax attacks, which convinced many Americans that the nation was under continuous assault. Letters containing anthrax were sent to Senators Leahy and Dashle, both potentiality instrumental in opposing the hastily passed Patriot Act. The FBI incorrectly blamed Bruce Ivins, resulting in his suicide. The FBI definitively determined that the anthrax spores originated at Fort Detrick in Maryland, one of many bio-weapons labs. But the original source material was ordered destroyed before the FBI investigation was completed.

• In 2003 Bush claimed non-existent "weapons of mass destruction" required the overthrow of Iraq's Saddam Hussein and continued presence in Afghanistan in wars that have claimed countless lives, cost hundreds of billions of dollars and thrown the entire Middle East into chaotic instability. Among the many explanations for why Bush attacked Iraq is the widespread belief that Presidential advisor

Karl Rove wanted it so the vastly unpopular Bush would be a "War President" while seeking re-election in 2004.

- President Obama later extended the war in Afghanistan, making it America's longest military intervention, a quagmire in which the US continues to strip Afghan "elections" of real public control in the interest of maintaining governments in Kabul friendly to the American military presence.

- In Libya, Syria and elsewhere, the US has become further embroiled in an endless morass of middle eastern regime changes, influenced and engineered with or without "elections" that continue to strip the region of peace and stability.

- In 2009, as then-Secretary of State, Hillary Clinton helped a right-wing coup in Honduras remove an elected leftist president, Manuel Zelaya, who was removed by force in the middle of the night and flown to Costa Rica. By her own admission, Clinton conspired to keep Zelaya from returning.

- The rise of terror organizations like ISIS and ISIL dedicated to psychotic acts of random murder, with no obvious goal or coherent strategy, and no easy off- switch, continues to shape our own elections as candidates outdo each other in demanding military solutions to complex problems where armed intervention often makes things worse.

Here the blowback to this long history of military interventions has left us with the world's largest, most expensive network of 900 military bases and US military personnel in as many as 175 countries. We now have a 200-year legacy of intrusion into the internal affairs of other nations, and a massive bureaucracy trained in making a mockery of the electoral process all around the world, including here.

As we'll see, this long history of unrestrained interventions has generated a massive body of technical expertise in overthrowing governments and rigging elections. It comes complete with a sense of entitlement and empowerment that – facilitated by electronic poll books and easily rigged voting machines – has flowed straight into stolen elections here at home.

In the next section of this book, we'll see how that expertise has come to bear in key locales like New Hampshire (1988), Florida (2000),

Ohio (2004), and maybe upcoming nationwide in 2016.

THE FIFTH JIM CROW:
Election Theft Comes To The US

As the troops returned home from World War II, and as the military and Major League Baseball were desegregated, a new level of technology entered the electoral playing field.

Overseas, the CIA began to apply advanced electronics to the art and science of election theft. By the 1970s, in front of the Church Committee, the Agency admitted to already having manipulated countless Third World elections to protect America's corporate and "national security" interests.

At home, powered in part by black veterans returning from WWII, Korea and then Vietnam, an increasingly effective Civil Rights Movement turned the African-American community into a rising nation-within-a-nation. Its demands for equal rights, including the right to vote, began to resemble the rise of other oppressed nations around the world. With the extraordinary leadership of Dr. Martin Luther King, Jr. and others, the movement became increasingly difficult for the powers to ignore.

Then, with John F. Kennedy, the Democratic Party shifted to the left on race. The black-white alliance so desperately feared by America's ruling elites for 300 years, began to take tangible shape in the wild tumult of the 1960s.

Paralleling what was being done to charismatic left leaders around the rest of the world, Medgar Evers, Malcolm X, JFK, Martin Luther King and Robert F. Kennedy were all assassinated.

Then, in 1971, Richard Nixon escalated the Republican Party's

"Southern Strategy" with a 45-year police action in the form of the Drug War, as described earlier.

But there were now additional new ways to fight black power. The use of electronics to overturn elections had been tried and tested overseas by the Central Intelligence Agency and other arms of the imperium.

Under Ronald Reagan, it became available for use in elections here at home. In 1988, former CIA director George H. W. Bush becomes the first to benefit:

- In 1950, the Bureau of Social Science Research (BSSR) was founded as a division of the School of Social Sciences and Public Affairs at the American University. In 1953, it became a non-profit organization involved with the CIA, and was used as a propaganda tool in the overthrow of Iran's Mossadegh. It then emerged as key player in the rise of electronic voting.

- In 1974, the US General Accounting Office commissioned a year-long study on the rise of electronic voting equipment. In 1975, Roy G. Saltman, an electronics expert at the National Bureau of Standards, warned about the dangers of electronic voting. In his *Effective Use of Computing Technology in Vote Counting*, he wrote: "Increasing computerization of election-related functions may result in the loss of effective controls over these functions by responsible authorities and that this loss of control may increase the possibility of vote fraud." (National Bureau of Standards Special Publication #500-30).

- In 1975, the CIA admitted to a US Senate investigative committee chaired by Senator Frank Church that it was engaged in 5000 "benign" operations, which involved, among other things, electronic election rigging in the Third World. Election theft was preferable to a bloody coup, said the Agency.

- In 1975 Congress created the Federal Election Commission (FEC).

- Gary Greenhalgh emerged as a key player as the assistant staff director at the FEC from May 1976 to January 1985. In 1983, he co-founded the International Center on Election Law & Administration to promote electronic voting worldwide. In 1985, he founded his own company, The Election Center, to promote electronic voting. In 1997, he became regional account manager for Election Systems &

Software (ES&S) which today controls almost 50% of the American vote, as the company Dominion, controls nearly the other half.

- In its coverage of the 1980 Iowa Republican Caucus, the *Manchester Union-Leader* (New Hampshire) wrote: "The Bush operation has all the smell of a CIA covert Operation….Strange aspects of the Iowa operation [include] a long, slow count and then the computers broke down at a very convenient point, with Bush having a 6% bulge over Reagan." Bush won the primary over Reagan, 31.6% to 21.5%. Bush declared he had the "Big Mo," i.e. momentum. This break-down of tabulating equipment at a key point in the vote count became a staple of the electronic tabulation process in elections to come.

- In 1981, the Reagan-Bush administration established ties between the Bureau of Social Science Research (BSSR) and the International Center for Election Law & Administration (ICELA). The CIA-linked BSSR provided initial funding for the ICELA to promote the spread of electronic voting machines worldwide.

- In 1984, at Greenhalgh's urging, the Election Center, affiliated with the Academy for State and Local Government, was established. The Center was an independent non-profit resource serving US state and local election officials. In 1985, Greenhalgh took over as director.

- In 1984, the *New York Times* revealed that a company called The Computer Election System of Berkeley, California, created a software program and related equipment "…used in more than a thousand county and local jurisdictions to collect and count 34.4 million of the 93.7 million votes cast in the United States," more than a third of the total votes. President Reagan signed National Security Directive NSDD245. The *New York Times* revealed that the secret directive involved: "a branch of the National Security Agency investigating whether a computer program that counted more than one-third of all the votes cast in the United States in 1984 is vulnerable to fraudulent manipulation."

- On December 18, 1985, legendary *New York Times* reporter David Burnham reported in California Official Investigating Computer Voting Security that state Attorney General John Van de Kamp found major errors in the computerized vote count from the 1984 election in California and elsewhere. Problems were found in at least thirteen areas nationwide, including Illinois, Montana and North

Dakota. Van de Kamp said he "is concerned about what he sees as a potentially serious problem."

- In 1985, Greenhalgh, who had become director of International Center on Election Law and Administration, stated that electronic voting presents "a massive potential for problems" and that it "centralizes the opportunity for fraud," according to the book by election integrity activist Bev Harris, Black Box Voting.

- On November 25, 1986, Dr. Michael Ian Shamos, a computer scientist employed by the Pennsylvania Bureau of Elections as an electronic voting systems examiner, issued a report entitled *An Outline of Testimony on Computer Voting Before the Texas Legislature.* His conclusion: "When one company or a conglomerate of companies apply unauditable software from a general distribution point, or participate directly in ballot setup procedures, there exists the possibility of large-scale tampering with elections. An errant programmer or tainted executive could influence or determine the outcome of a majority of election precincts in a country...."

- The July 21, 1986 issue of *Election Administration Reports* (#80), a newsletter for election administration officials, in reference to a disputed 1986 Democratic primary for County Commissioner in Stark County, Ohio, concluded: "A special computer program was written, in order to count only the disputed contest and not the other contests on the ballot. The mystery, however, was why 165 additional votes had been tallied in the recount, although the number of ballots read by the computer was the same.....A more complete checkout using a large number of ballots would have identified the logical error that caused the program used in the recount to fail to distinguish between voters of different political parties." In other words, the program awarded Republican votes to certain Democrats, a syndrome that would resurface in the stolen presidential election in Ohio in 2004.

- In 1987, Greenhalgh resigned as director of the Election Center to become vice president of operations for the R.F. Shoup Company. The company's founder, Ransom Shoup, had been convicted in 1979 for conspiring to defraud the federal government in connection with a bribe attempt to obtain voting machine business, according to the *Commercial Appeal* newspaper of Memphis. His machines were known as Shouptronics. Under a different name, these machines were used in the disputed 2004 election in Columbus, Ohio.

- In 1987, Carol Garner became the Election Center's second director. She had previously worked for Governor Bill Clement of Texas and was an associate of Karl Rove, who worked for Clement in the 1978 gubernatorial campaign.

- In the 1988, New Hampshire Republican primary, the nation witnessed the first large-scale use of computer voting machines in a presidential election. Former CIA Director George H.W. Bush trailed Bob Dole by eight points in polls taken on Election Day. But when the votes were electronically tallied, Bush beat Dole by nine points. Such a 17-point turn-around qualifies among mainstream election statistical analysts as a "virtual statistical impossibility."

- In August, 1988, Roy Saltman wrote *Accuracy, Integrity and Security in Computerized Vote Tallying* for the National Bureau of Standard's Institute for Computer Sciences and Technology. He warned that "the possibility that unknown persons may perpetrate undiscoverable frauds" was a key problem with electronic voting systems.

- In 1988 Ronnie Dugger, long-time editor of the *Texas Observer*, wrote a major piece on the move toward electronic-based elections in the *New Yorker Magazine*. He warned that the capacity now exists for "...altering the computer program or the control punch cards that manipulate it, planting a time bomb, manually removing an honest counting program, and replacing it with a fraudulent one, counting fake ballots, altering the vote recorder that voters use at the polls or changing either the logic that controls precinct-located vote-counting devices, or the voting summaries in these units' removable data-hyphen storage unit." Dugger concluded: "the problem in this segment of the computer business, as in the field at large, is not only invisibility but also information as electricity."

- In 1996, Chuck Hagel ran for US Senate in Nebraska against popular incumbent Democratic Governor Ben Nelson. Hagel had never held elective office. But he was part-owner of ES&S, a computerized voting machine company whose machines were used in conducting the statewide election. Michael McCarthy, president of ES&S, was Hagel's campaign treasurer. Hagel became Nebraska's first Republican elected to the US Senate in 24 years. Hagel's part ownership of ES&S was hidden from the public during the campaign. One Nebraska newspaper called Hegel's victory a "stunning upset." Some 80% of the state's ballots were cast and counted on ES&S machines.

The Electronic Selection of 2000

In 2000, Democrat Al Gore, the incumbent Vice President, won the nationwide presidential vote tally by more than 500,000 votes.

But for the first time since 1876, a Constitutional crisis arose over the alignment of the Electoral College. The final decision was thrown to the state of Florida (which had also been "in play" in 1876).

The Bush campaign was coordinated by Karl Rove. The Florida election was officially controlled by Republican Secretary of State Katherine Harris, who openly supported Bush as the co-chair of his election campaign.

The GOP campaign employed a wide range of tactics reminiscent of the Jim Crow era to cut into the turnout among tens of thousands blacks and Latinos, who favored Gore by as much as 9:1. Among other things, state police and other law enforcement agencies physically intimidated potential voters in predominantly black areas of Orlando and elsewhere.

In largely Jewish areas of south Florida, where Gore and his vice-presidential candidate Joe Lieberman campaigned repeatedly, misleading "butterfly ballots" yielded large numbers of votes for Pat Buchanan, who is widely viewed as anti-Semitic. Many Jewish residents later realized votes they thought they had cast for Gore went to Buchanan instead, becoming the subject of Aviva Kempner's classic documentary "Today I Voted for My Joey."

In other predominantly Democratic areas around the state, shortages of voting machines and a lack of paper ballots slashed Gore's vote count.

Nonetheless, early Election Day evening, exit polls and preliminary vote counts showed Gore as the clear winner. But a Constitutional crisis arose as the vote count suddenly became an extremely tight vote. The entire fiasco is based largely on complications with the electronic voter registration and voting process:

- As the Florida polls closed, major networks reported that Al Gore was the winner. But as the count proceeded, the Fox network suddenly reported that Florida was "in play."

- A vote count "glitch" on Global Election Systems (later Diebold) machines in Volusia County, Florida, subtracted 16,022 votes from Gore, and added 4,000 votes for George W. Bush. Bush's first cousin John Ellis, who had been hired as a Fox Network temporary election analyst, used the shift to proclaim that his cousin would win Florida and the presidency.

- Bev Harris, author of *Black Box Voting*, posted a series of internal Diebold memos relating to the Volusia County miscount on her website, blackboxvoting.com. One memo from Lana Hires of Global Election Systems, now part of Diebold, complained, "I need some answers! Our department is being audited by the County. I have been waiting for someone to give me an explanation as to why Precinct 216 gave Al Gore a minus 16,022 [votes] when it was uploaded." Another, from Talbot Ireland, Senior VP of Research and Development for Diebold, referred to key "replacement" votes in Volusia County as "unauthorized."

- Based on exclusive reporting by Bev Harris of Black Box Voting, and by award-winning journalist Greg Palast, *The Nation* magazine reported that Florida Governor Jeb Bush (brother of GOP candidate George W. Bush) electronically purged Florida's voter registration lists in a partisan manner. He used a secret proprietary computer program from a $4 million contract with Database Technologies (DBT) recently merged with ChoicePoint Inc. of Atlanta, which was the only bidder, to coordinate the definitive electronic purge. ChoicePoint has strong right-wing ties among its Board of Directors.

- The contract was awarded in 1998 by a Republican legislature in league with then-Secretary of State Sandra Mortham, who later became Jeb Bush's Lieutenant Governor. That August, Mortham was warned by the Florida State Association of Supervisors of Elections that there was a botched rush "to capriciously take names off the rolls."

- The purge involved 90,000 or more duly registered Florida voters, very far more than the 537 votes that allegedly decided the election for George W. Bush.

- The purge affected primarily black and Latino citizens who vote overwhelmingly Democratic, and who would easily have turned the election to Gore.

- The DBT list included thousands of citizens who had allegedly been convicted of felonies, but actually were not.

- Many of the names on the DBT purge list came from other states, such as Alabama. There, a "John Jones" may have been convicted of a felony, while the "John Jones" in Florida was not, but the Florida John Jones was purged from the registration books anyway. In many cases, differing middle initials were ignored, as were differing suffixes such as "Junior" and "III." Many such misidentified citizens had been lawfully registered for years and showed up to vote on November 7 at their traditional precincts but were told they were not registered and were not allowed to vote.

- Many of the names on the DBT purge list were those of citizens who may have been felons in other states but had since moved to Florida, where their right to vote was not legally deniable. According to Palast's report, criminal demographer Jeffrey Manza of Northwestern University said at least 80% of such citizens should have been legally granted the right to vote in Florida. But they were denied anyway. The number of rightfully eligible Florida voters purged based on names coming from Texas, Ohio and Illinois were, each on their own, sufficient to turn the election.

- Palast reported that David Bositis, senior research associate at the Joint Center for Political and Economic Studies in Washington, DC, described the purge as "a patently obvious technique to discriminate against black voters." Blacks, he said, would account for nearly half the "ex-felons" wrongly denied their vote.

- In Hillsborough County, Florida, election supervisors confirmed that 54% of the lawful voters electronically denied their vote were black in a county where blacks comprised just 11% of the voting population.

- Overall, DBT electronically "scrubbed" nearly 3,000 voters based on alleged felonies once possibly committed (or not at all) by citizens who came into Florida from at least eight states where their voting rights would have been automatically restored prior to coming to the Sunshine State.

- One electronically scrubbed voter was Pastor Thomas Johnson of Gainesville, Florida. Johnson was pastor of the House of Hope, a faith-based charity that guided ex-convicts from jail into a working life. The program was praised by Johnson's personal friend, Jeb Bush. Nonetheless, Pastor Johnson was denied the right to vote based on a New York felony from a previous decade.

- The electronic purge proceeded despite previous federal court decisions ruling it illegal. Ultimately, the purge was key to putting George W. Bush in the White House.

- Amidst a global media tsunami, "hanging chads" and other problems complicated the election recount. Violent (but well-dressed) GOP operatives stormed election boards in what were known as the "Brooks Brothers Riots." Election officials were intimated and the process slowed, deepening the sense of a national crisis.

- Amidst the chaos the crisis was "solved" by an inexplicable 5-4 vote of the US Supreme Court which stopped the recount and handed the presidency to George W. Bush. The Justices called this Bush v. Gore landmark a "one-time only" decision, not meant to set precedent. At least one pro-Bush Justice, Sandra Day O'Connor, later regretted her vote.

- The Congressional Black Caucus appeared before the Senate where Gore was the presiding officer and attempted to challenge the Florida electoral vote but at Gore's request, the Senate refused to allow it to be considered. Hillary Clinton told the *Free Press* that she wished the election would have been challenged.

- A year later, more thorough recounts of the Florida vote were conducted by an independent media consortium. If the 175,000 so-called "spoiled ballots" had been counted, Gore would have won by approximately 29,000 votes.

- In his later film *An Inconvenient Truth*, Gore jokingly mentioned that he was once "the next president of the United States." But he did nothing to further research or publicize what actually happened in Florida and around the US with the electronic vote count and other irregularities that denied the will of the voting public and changed the course of history.

- Post-2000 corporate media coverage largely blamed independent candidate Ralph Nader for turning the election from Gore to Bush. The media and Democratic mainstream ignored the fact that Gore actually won the election both in Florida and nationwide, but was deprived of the presidency by Jim Crow intimidation and electronic theft. Neither Gore nor the Democrats took effective steps to address either of these problems in the four-year lead-up to the next presidential election....or any time since.

The Help American Vote Act of 2002

- In 2002, the Congress responded to the Florida fiasco by passing the Help America Vote Act (HAVA), providing billions in federal funding for states to shift the registration and voting process onto electronic machines.

- In 2002, Republican Nebraska Senator Chuck Hagel was "re-elected" with more than 80% of the vote. Hagel was still a principle in the ES&S electronic voting machine company. The state's votes were cast and counted in large part on machines in which the candidate had a financial share. His official margin of victory was highly improbable, because he received an unexpectedly high vote among urban and black voters.

- In the November 2002 Georgia election, incumbent US Senator Max Cleland lost his seat against Saxby Chambliss in an unexpected last-minute upset. It was the first election in which Georgia had used Diebold voting machines, and just prior to Election Day in an unusual move, the president of Diebold's election unit Bob Urosevich brought in illegal software updates to the system. Bev Harris of Black Box Voting found a set of files called "rob-georgia" among the secret voting machine database files.

- In the 2002 Alabama gubernatorial election, Bob Riley (R) defeated sitting governor Don Siegelman (D) by the smallest margin in Alabama history – some 3000 votes. Siegelman was one of the most popular politicians in Alabama's history, the only one elected to the top four statewide offices from Secretary of State, Attorney General, Lieutenant Governor to Governor. The Associated Press initially declared Siegelman the winner on election night. In Baldwin County, Alabama the paper ballots had been opti-scanned and the results posted. During the wee hours, the posted results showed an unexplained shift that supposedly produced enough additional votes to give Riley the election. Siegelman's campaign wanted to count the paper ballots from Baldwin County to determine the real results, but Alabama's Republican Attorney General Bill Pryor refused to allow the disputed votes from the malfunctioning machine to be manually recounted. He impounded the paper ballots from Baldwin County and said he would criminally prosecute anyone who tried to get their hands on them effectively ending the election dispute over the vote count.

- In 2006, Siegelman was sentenced to seven years in prison after being convicted on felony corruption charges. More than 100 former Attorney Generals and government officials in both major parties have alleged that Siegelman's conviction was politically motivated and marred by prosecutorial misconduct. Dana Jill Simpson, a Republican lawyer and political operative, swore under oath that she was on a conference call with Karl Rove when he orchestrated criminal charges against Siegelman to neutralize him in Alabama. Raw Story reported that Rove worked with Bill Canary, Alabama's top Republican operative. The voting machine controversy and conviction ended Siegelman's political career.

The "All the Above" Selection of 2004

As the election of 2004 approached, incumbent President George W. Bush seemed unlikely to win a second term. His performance in the wake of the 9/11 attacks won him many supporters. But as time passed, his failure to protect the country from those attacks and much else about his presidency, affirmed for others an impression of profound incompetence, even of conspiracy.

In August 2002, presidential advisor Karl Rove established and chaired the White House Iraq Group (WHIG). Its mission was to develop a strategy for publicizing the White House's assertion that Saddam Hussein posed a threat to the United States.

In 2003, presidential advisor Karl Rove calculated that Bush's chance to win a second term would be improved if he could call himself a "War President." So Rove, Vice-President Dick Cheney and other hawks within the administration began to promote an all-out assault on Iraq, which by all accounts had nothing to do with the attack on the World Trade Center.

The attack was sold with the clam that Iraqi dictator Saddam Hussein (originally installed by the CIA, and publicly embraced in the 1980s by Secretary of Defense Donald Rumsfeld) had weapons of mass destruction. The assertion was false.

The war was cheer-led in large part by Cheney, who predicted that the Iraqi people would shower American soldiers with love and flowers as they invaded. This preposterous ideological line was sold to the US electorate by a small neo-conservative think tank called the Project for a New American Century.

Instead the invasion opened a Pandora's Box of instability and bloodshed. Hundreds of thousands of Iraqis died, along with thousands of US soldiers. The invasion cost hundreds of billions of dollars and spawned a network of global terror that has extended from Al Quaeda to ISIS and beyond.

As the war grew increasingly unpopular, all predictions of the 2004 electoral outcome hinged on Ohio, Pennsylvania and Florida. We have documented more than 100 of these in our How The GOP Stole America's 2004 Election…which was published in 2005. (see it at www.freepress.org).

OHIO
The 2004 Presidential Election

- In March 2004, Bob Fitrakis and Harvey Wasserman published the article *Diebold, Electronic Voting, and the Vast Right-Wing Conspiracy* on freepress.org and on motherjones.com predicting that Ohio would be the new Florida in the 2004 presidential election because of the partisan connections of George W. Bush to the private owners of the electronic voting machines and vote tabulation software. The key source for the article, Athan Gibbs, was an African American entrepreneur who had invented a voting machine that gave each voter a verified voting receipt. Approximately one week after the article ran, Gibbs was killed when his car was hit by a truck on an interstate highway.

- Due in part to the Help America Vote Act (HAVA), like most of the rest of the country, the majority of Ohio's 2004 registration records were managed electronically, and votes were cast and counted electronically.

- In Auglaize County, the whistle-blowing Deputy Director of the Board of Elections resigned after complaining that a former employee of ES&S was given "inappropriate" access to voting machines prior to Election Day.

- On Election Day 2004, virtually all Ohio's votes were tabulated on electronic machines owned by companies with strong Republican ties, including Diebold, ES&S (with ties to Chuck Hagel), and Triad.

- In 2002, Tom Noe, Chair of the Lucas County (Toledo) Board of Elections, had brought in Sequoia touchscreen machines. But the county used O'Dell's Diebold machines during the 2004 election. Neither offers an independently monitored paper trail for verifying election outcomes.

- Noe was later convicted of laundering money into the Bush re-election campaign in a scandal involving ties with Republican Governor Bob Taft, who allowed the state to make fraudulent investments in Noe's coin business.

- Tom Noe was succeeded as Chair of the Lucas County Board of Elections by his wife Bernadette. During the 2004 election process, she allowed GOP election officials access to unsecured ballots into an area designated as requiring both a Democrat and Republican to be present together.

- Under Bernadette Noe's leadership, the County's Diebold electronic voting machines broke down before Election Day and remained in disrepair throughout the November 7 election, disenfranchising thousands of voters.

- In 2003, Ohio businessman Walden "Wally" O'Dell, promised in a fund raising letter to wealthy GOP supporters that he would deliver Ohio's electoral votes to Bush. O'Dell ran Diebold, which owned and operated the bulk of Ohio's electronic voting machines. Diebold also controlled the software that would count the votes that decided the 2004 presidential election.

- O'Dell had visited the president's ranchette – a converted pig farm – in Crawford, Texas, and was a "Bush Ranger" responsible for delivering more than $100,000 to the Bush/Cheney/Rove campaign for a second term. O'Dell hosted at least one Bush fundraiser with an admission price of $1,000 per guest. Except for the *Columbus Free*

Press, no national or Ohio media found this conflict of interest worth noting.

- Ohio's Secretary of State in 2004 was J. Kenneth Blackwell, who played a role parallel to that played by Kathleen Harris in Florida 2000. The central part of Blackwell's job was to administer the state's elections. He simultaneously co-chaired Ohio's GOP committee to give Bush and Cheney a second term, a re-run of Katherine Harris's dual role in Florida 2000.

- Blackwell was a far-right Republican known for his outspoken contempt for those who disagreed with him. He administered Ohio's election using an "all the above" barrage of tactics pioneered throughout the Third World by the CIA and other covert operatives since the beginning of the Cold War.

- To count the votes, Blackwell awarded a no-bid contract to GovTech, an Akron-based IT firm owned by Michael Connell, a long-time Bush family operative. Connell had created the Bush-Cheney website for the 2000 presidential campaign. As a chief IT consultant and operative for Karl Rove, Connell was a devout Catholic and the father of four children. In various statements Connell cited his belief that abortion is murder as a primary motivating factor in his work for the Republican Party and his strong desire to see candidates who supported legal abortion be defeated.

- Connell's company, New Media Communications worked closely with SmartTech in building Republican and right-wing websites that were hosted on SmartTech servers. Among Connell's clients were the Republican National Committee, Swift Boat Veterans for Truth and gwb43.com. The SmartTech servers at one point housed Karl Rove's emails. Some of Rove's email files have since mysteriously disappeared despite repeated Congressional and court-sanctioned attempts to review them.

- In 2001, Michael Connell's GovTech Solutions, LLC was selected to reorganize the Capitol Hill IT network, the only private-sector company to gain permission from HIR (House Information Resources) to place its server behind the firewall, he bragged.

- Prior to the election, Blackwell established a wide range of measures aimed at systematically disenfranchising potential Democratic voters, and for electronically shifting the vote count to guarantee a

Bush-Cheney victory.

- Ohio's system of elections provided that each county board of elections have two Democrats and two Republicans, with the Secretary of State's vote as the tie-breaker, meaning all 88 counties in 2004 were controlled by Blackwell.

- In the lead up to the vote, Blackwell eliminated numerous precincts from inner city Democrat-leaning areas. He consolidated them into larger precincts, causing procedures on Election Day to be more difficult and suppression of the black vote became much easier. Few precincts were eliminated in the state's rural Republican areas. Similar maneuvers have become commonplace throughout our elections, including the infamous Arizona primary in 2016, where voters in largely Latino areas waited five hours and more to cast their ballots.

- As precincts were shifted, the Ohio Secretary of State's website had out-of-date inaccurate information, frequently directing citizens to places where they would not be able vote, or where provisional ballots would be required.

- A Hocking County, Ohio board official leaked information to the *Free Press* that Lisa Schwartze, GOP-appointed Director of the Hocking County Board of Elections, shredded voter registration documents prior to the 2004 election.

- The Lucas County (Toledo) Democratic Party headquarters was burglarized, with loss of crucial voter lists, internal correspondence and other campaign documents just prior to election.

- More than 30,000 letters on official boards of elections stationery throughout southern Ohio were sent to alleged ex-felons threatening them with arrest if they attempted to vote, even though there was no law in Ohio preventing ex-felons from voting.

- Eleven months before the 2004 election, Matt Damschroder, the GOP Director of the Franklin County (Columbus) Board of Elections, accepted a $10,000 donation from Diebold contractor Pasquale "Patsy" Gallina on behalf of the county's Republican Party. Damschroder was suspended without pay for a month.

- Blackwell demanded Ohio's 88 counties print all voter registration forms on 80 bond paper or they would be rejected, but the ones distributed from his own office were on 60 bond paper and would have been rejected under his decree.

- Operatives of unknown origin went door-to-door "registering" potential inner city voters, then trashing the forms, rendering the signees ineligible to vote. They also picked up absentee ballots from nursing homes that never made it to the boards of elections. Such "caging" tactics were illegal, but were rampant throughout the state during the 2004 election.

- Prior to the 2004 election, more than 300,000 voters were purged from the registration rolls, virtually all of them in heavily Democratic urban areas such as Cleveland, Cincinnati, and Columbus. (Bush's official margin of victory was less than 118,775). They were purged without explanation in a presidential election year, when voter purges did not normally occur in Ohio.

- In Lucas County, Board Chair Bernadette Noe purged some 28,000 voters from registration rolls, including some who'd voted in the same precinct, without changing residence, for four decades.

- Throughout the state, duly registered voters (including co-author Harvey Wasserman) were denied absentee ballots.

- On Election Day, President Bush and Rove personally visited Blackwell at Republican headquarters in Columbus. The meeting was secret. Bush gave no public speeches in Ohio that day, but did make a "get out the vote" call.

- Blackwell banned international election observers from coming within 100 feet of Ohio's polling places. He threatened to arrest a distinguished United Nations team if they tried to do any monitoring inside any Ohio precinct. Such actions would have been roundly condemned by US democracy advocates monitoring election rights in other countries.

- However, Blackwell did allow Republican "challengers" into primarily African-American precincts to threaten potential voters with Jim Crow-style retribution if their voter registrations were not "in order."

- For the first time in Ohio's history, Blackwell imposed a wide range of very restrictive management policies, including a refusal to count ballots for president cast by a voter in a precinct other than the one in which s/he was registered. This included denying voting rights to citizens who came to the right building to vote, but mistakenly lined up at the wrong table in a crowded general voting area, even if the right table was next to it, less than a three feet away.

- Blackwell refused to provide paper ballots as requested even by Republican officials in the event machines broke down.

- Registration books at numerous precincts were out-of-date, disenfranchising thousands of Ohioans, especially in Franklin County.

- The Franklin County (Columbus) Board of Elections requested 5,000 new machines for Election Day. But, Blackwell vetoed the purchase of the new machines. Thus, the election was conducted with a roughly half the number needed. The shortages were primarily in Democratic precincts. The resulting long lines made it impossible for many working citizens to vote.

- In Franklin County, 76 wards had fewer voting machines available on November 2nd than they had during the spring primary election. All 76 wards that were shorted on machines were in the city of Columbus, rather than in the suburbs; 42 of the short-changed precincts were in predominantly African-American districts. Statewide shortages and misallocation of voting machines and other impediments led to long delays, that, when combined with an atmosphere of intimidation and other problems, may have prompted 3% of the state's electorate to be disenfranchised, representing a vote total well in excess of Bush's official margin of victory.

- The machine shortages caused long lines in numerous precincts, most of them predominantly African-American. In the inner city of Columbus, wait times for voting were 3-7 hours.

- Some absentee ballots were delivered pre-punched for George W. Bush.

- Thousands of absentee ballots did not arrive for Ohio citizens (as in Florida) until after Election Day.

- In Hamilton County (Cincinnati) some absentee ballots were delivered lacking an option to vote for John Kerry.

- As with butterfly ballots used in Florida 2000, absentee ballots in Ohio 2004 were often impossible to understand or deliberately confusing.

- The Republican Party sent thousands of letters to college students challenging their right to vote based on their residency.

- Republican Director of the Franklin County Board of Elections, Matt Damschroder sent letters to ex-felons, felons, and those charged with felonies or misdemeanors, and to many citizens who turned out to have no criminal record whatsoever. The letters wrongly warned the recipients that they had lost their right to vote and that they would be arrested if they tried to do so.

- Ex-felons, people behind on their child support and people traffic tickets were targeted with threatening phone calls by a Republican "Mighty Texas Task Force" made up of GOP operatives who flew into the state for the election, warning these Ohio citizens not to vote or they would be arrested.

- Disinformational flyers were circulated in inner-city precincts on official-looking stationary threatening civil rights and voter registration groups with legal prosecution if they helped citizens register to vote.

- Flyers on official-looking stationary were circulated in inner cities advising Democrats to vote the day after the election. They read: "Due to increased voter registration, Republicans vote on Tuesday and Democrats will vote on Wednesday."

- Voters in crowded inner city voting precincts were forced to use provisional ballots if they came to the "wrong" table, even if the "right" table was two feet away, or they had to go back to the end of the "right" line.

- Cars legally parked at inner city precincts were illegally towed while their owners attempted to vote in very long lines caused by shortages of machines and time-consuming harassment by GOP challengers.

- Citizens waiting in line to vote when their precincts closed at 7:30pm were illegally ordered to leave without voting; the law provided that those in line when the precincts closed were entitled to vote even after closing time.

- In Knox County, students at Kenyon College and local citizens were forced to wait up to 12 hours to vote due to a shortage of working machines and a lack of paper ballots, while students at a nearby fundamentalist Bible college waited just five minutes to vote.

- Students at Oberlin College and citizens of Oberlin, a liberal bastion, waited eight hours to vote due to an "unavoidable" shortage of machines and Blackwell's refusal to provide paper ballots.

- At Wilberforce College, mostly African-American students were illegally challenged during the registration process.

- In Lucas County, the wrong ballot marking pens were issued for opti-scan voting cards which did not register on the machines designated to read them, thus creating thousands of "spoiled ballots" that were never counted.

- Blackwell failed to provide Spanish-speaking poll workers as required by law in heavily Latino precincts, especially in Cleveland.

- The implausibility of the vote count was confirmed in part by official vote tallies in key southwestern Ohio counties showing Kerry being credited with far fewer votes than those counted for C. Ellen Connelly, a black Democrat running for the Ohio Supreme Court. Connelly never campaigned in the heavily white rural area and was virtually unknown there. The idea that she would receive more votes than Kerry is highly improbable.

- In Mahoning County (Youngstown), voting machines were recalibrated in the middle of Election Day, creating long lines and casting doubt on the vote count. Between twenty and thirty ES&S iVotronic machines broke down in the middle of the voting process and had to be re-calibrated because voters were complaining that they tried to vote for one candidate but the machine indicated that a vote for a different candidate was being recorded. The Mahoning County Board of Elections admitted that 31 of their voting machines were flipping votes.

- In sworn testimony taken after the election, voters in Mahoning County reported pushing John Kerry's name on their touchscreen voting machines and having George W. Bush's name light up. In sworn testimony after the election, one voter said this "vote hopping" happened repeatedly on his machine, and that an election official confirmed that it had been doing that "all day." The poll worker suggested he just keep pushing Kerry's name until it stuck.

- Voters in Franklin County reported seeing their vote for Kerry disappear from the voting machine screen. This became known as the "Franklin County Fade."

- On election night, immediately after the polls closed, Warren County GOP officials inexplicably declared a Level 10 Homeland Security alert and excluded all media observers from the vote count. All materials relating to the vote count were confiscated by GOP officials, who ordered media representatives out of the process, in contradiction to long-standing practice. They moved the ballots from an officially sanctioned site to an unsanctioned warehouse, raising suspicions about the validity of the chain of command. Later investigations indicate that before Election Day, discussions had occurred in Warren County election circles about the possibility of a Homeland Security alert during the vote count. But no confirmation of any authorization of such an alert ever came from the FBI or any other federal agency that might have been authorized to call one. To this day, Warren County officials have issued no documented explanation for the origin of the Homeland Security alert. Despite exit polls indicating he received fewer votes, Bush was credited with 14,000 more votes than he had received in 2000.

- The "Loaves and Fishes" vote count in Gahanna, a Columbus suburb inside Franklin County, gave Bush an impossible tally. At the Ward 1B precinct in Gahanna, a suburb of Columbus, 4,258 votes were tallied for George W. Bush where only 638 people were registered. The precinct was housed at the New Life Church, a fundamentalist congregation led by cohorts of the Rev. Jerry Falwell, a close associate of George W. Bush. The glitch was blamed on a faulty electronic transmission, but was later dubbed the "loaves and fishes" vote count, in Falwell's honor.

- Two strongly pro-Bush precincts in Perry County initially reported official voter turnouts in excess of 100%. They reported turnouts of 124.4% and 124.0% respectively. The vote count was heavily in favor of George W. Bush.

- The vote count in two strongly pro-Bush Miami County precincts reported impossibly high results. The tallies in the Concord South and Southwest precincts of Miami County reported official turnouts of 94.27% and 98.6% respectively. The vote counts were strongly in favor of Bush. County election officials later admitted that there were approximately 2500 phantom cyber-votes added to their vote tally by the central tabulators.

- On Election night, GOP-controlled Miami County announced a total turnout of 31,620 votes, with a majority of about 66% favoring George W. Bush. Later, the Board of Elections added nearly 19,000 votes to the total, about 13,000 of which went to Bush. The second tabulation gave John Kerry precisely the same percentage of the vote as the first one, another virtual statistical impossibility.

- A faulty electronic voting machine in Mahoning County (Youngstown) showed John Kerry receiving a negative 25,000,000 votes. The "glitch" was apparently "corrected."

- Republican-controlled Warren, Butler and Clermont Counties gave Bush a total margin of victory over Kerry in excess of his entire margin in the state of Ohio and in excess of what he got in 2000 over Al Gore. Official tallies showed Bush beating John Kerry by a collective margin of 132,685 votes in Warren, Butler and Clermont Counties. Bush's margin in these three counties alone substantially exceeded his 118,775-vote margin of victory in the entire state.

- In Trumbull County, which went heavily for Bush, 650 more absentee ballots were counted than there were absentee voters. (In Broward and Palm Beach Counties, Florida, problems with absentee ballots had also cost tens of thousands of citizens their right to vote.)

- After the election, Blackwell illegally ordered all poll records to be kept secret from the public, with at least one volunteer election monitor being physically ejected in Pickaway County.

- Minor, obscure third-party candidates got unexplained, improbable high vote counts in a few Cuyahoga County precincts that vote heavily Democratic, denying those votes to Kerry. Results showed that Black neighborhoods voted inexplicably for the far right-wing Constitutional Law Party.

- At least seven heavily Democratic precincts in Cleveland showed voter turnouts 30% lower than the average in the rest of the state for no apparent reason, costing Kerry thousands of votes.

- In Democratic-rich northern Ohio including Toledo and Cleveland, the ratio of machine-rejected ballots versus those successfully counted was eight times higher in Democratic precincts than in Republican precincts.

- In some areas, underfunded and little-known "down-ballot" Democratic candidates received more votes than the presidential candidate John Kerry, a highly unlikely outcome. Kerry also received, in certain Republican-controlled areas, fewer votes in the November election than he got in the spring primary that had a much lighter voter turnout

- In Greene County, bags of official ballots were left unguarded on folding tables in an open building, breaking the chain of command and compromising any recount.

- In one Lucas County (Toledo) precinct, zero voting machines were available to the public at the beginning of the day, depriving many citizens of their ability to vote.

- In Lucas County down-ballot congressional Democratic candidate Marcy Kaptur was credited with 13,461 more votes than Kerry.

- In Mahoning County (Youngstown) voting machines were re-calibrated in the middle of Election Day, creating long lines and eradicating the reliability of the vote count.

- Voters in Mahoning and Franklin counties using touch-screen machines repeatedly reported pushing Kerry's name on the screen while having Bush light up. In some cases pushing Kerry's name would bring on a light that would then fade away, apparently leaving no vote being cast.

- Mike Connell set up the vote-counting apparatus for Ohio's election results in the basement of the Old Pioneer Bank Building in Chattanooga, Tennessee.

- At 12:20am on the night of the 2004 presidential election, when election exit polls and initial vote counts showed John Kerry the clear winner, the Ohio computers went down and the state's vote counting was moved to Tennessee. Blackwell had dismissed state IT workers for the night, leaving the vote count in this historically critical period under the supervision of Michael Connell.

- At 12:30am, CNN reported that John Kerry was carrying Ohio with a margin of 4.2% (more than 200,000 votes) and would almost certainly become the next President.

- Around 2am the computers came back up and the vote count had shifted, giving Bush the presidency. Kerry's 4.2% margin of victory shifted to a 2.5% margin of victory for Bush.

- This shift of 6.7% (more than 300,000 votes) has been termed a "virtual statistical impossibility" by Dr. Ron Baiman, professor and statistician, and others.

- About 15% of the 5.6 million votes cast in the Ohio election were recorded by electronic voting machines that had no paper trails and could not be reliably monitored or recounted. This represented about 700,000 votes in an election whose official margin for George W. Bush was 118,775 votes. The reversal of a small percentage of the votes cast on electronic machines could have changed the outcome of the election. A shift of a mere six votes in each of Ohio's 11,000-plus precincts would have given Kerry the White House.

Post 2004 Ohio Election

- The source code for electronic machines has been ruled proprietary by the courts. There is still no way to cross-check or verify the electronic vote count from the disputed 2004 election or any other election held in Ohio or any other state where electronic voting has dominated.

- On a state-by-state basis, the Edison/Mitofsky and other major polling reports showed a strong correspondence between the exit polls and the official vote counts in 38 states plus the District of Columbia, with significant statistical variations concentrated in four key swing states: Florida, Ohio, Pennsylvania and New Hampshire.

- On election night 2004, Jonathan Simon, a lawyer and chiropractor, became the man who captured the screenshots of the national presidential election exit polls. Mitofsky International and Edison Media Research under contract to six major news organizations had conducted the exit polls. The screenshots captured by Simon documented an unexplained "Red Shift" in 10 out of the 11 swing states. The unexpected and improbable shifts all went toward George W. Bush. Simon would later write an important book on the topic, Code Red.

- Of America's eleven key swing states, ten experienced similar shifts from Kerry to Bush from 12:30am to the morning after the election. Wisconsin stayed steady for Kerry at 0.4%. Colorado and Florida started with slight leads for Bush and ended with large ones. Michigan, Minnesota, New Hampshire and Pennsylvania started with large leads for Kerry and ended with smaller ones. Iowa, Nevada, New Mexico and Ohio, all showed significant leads for Kerry at 12:30am; they all ended in the morning in the Bush column, giving him a second term. Those four "purple states," which shifted from blue to red, experienced shifts of 2.2%, 3.9%, 3.7% and, in Ohio, 6.7%.

- On November 13, 2004, the Ohio Election Protection coalition chaired by Bob Fitrakis, Free Press Editor and attorney, held the largest known public hearings about election and voting irregularities in Ohio history putting 32 Ohio precinct judges, pollworkers, legal observers, party challengers, voters and observers under oath. Additionally, 66 others provided written affidavits that day. Other hearings followed in Cincinnati, Toledo, Youngstown and another in Columbus. More than 500 people provided sworn testimony under oath on election irregularities. Their testimony provided the basis for the lawsuit Moss v. Bush.

- After the election, the presidential candidates from the national Green and Libertarian Parties filed for a recount of the vote in Ohio. Despite paying for the recount, they were denied the right to inspect poll books.

- Under Ohio law, recounts involve randomly counting 3% of the ballots in a county by hand and if they don't match, then all ballots are hand-counted. During the Ohio recount, precincts to be examined were specifically designated by Blackwell rather than being chosen at random.

- During the recount, Shelby and other Ohio counties discarded key equipment and data prior to being independently examined.

- In Hocking County during the recount, a representative of Triad, a conservative-owned voting machine company, replaced the county board of elections' central tabulator's hard drive and gave Deputy Director Sherole Eaton, a "cheat sheet" to use if the votes didn't match up. When Eaton made this information public, she was fired.

- In Ohio, Kerry carried 54.46% of the votes that were counted by hand during the recount.

- In the aftermath of the massive irregularities in the Ohio 2004 presidential election, Bill Moss, long-time black activist and former Columbus School Board member, contested the election results by filing an action before the Supreme Court of Ohio, *Moss v. Bush*. Due to the delays caused primarily by Ohio Secretary of State Blackwell, there was never a full hearing granted on the case. However, more than 20,000 pages documenting Ohio election irregularities and fraud were placed in the court record.

- US Congressman John Conyers of the House Judiciary Committee received so many complaints about election irregularities in Ohio that he held hearings in both Washington DC and Columbus, Ohio in December 2004. The information gathered at the hearings and through investigation by the Judiciary staff was published as a book entitled, *What Went Wrong in Ohio: The Conyers Report on the 2004 Election*. Noted literary figure Gore Vidal wrote the introduction.

- On December 13, 2004 before a hearing organized by US Rep John Conyers (D-MI) in Columbus, Ohio, computer programmer Clint Curtis testified that he was asked by US Rep. Tom Feeney (R-FL) to write a program for a touchscreen voting machine that would make it possible to flip votes without being detected.

- For the first time in US history, the entire electoral delegation of a state, Ohio, was challenged before the US Congress January 5, 2005. US Representative Stephanie Tubbs Jones (D-OH) of Cleveland, the first black female to serve as a House representative in Ohio, brought a formal complaint before the US Senate. US Senator Barbara Boxer (D-CA) provided the required support to allow it to be debated for two hours in both the House and the Senate. The challenge failed.

- Kerry conceded the 2004 election at 1pm the day after Election Day, despite the fact that 250,000 votes remain uncounted in Ohio, far in excess of the then-predicted Bush victory of 130,000 (it came in finally at 118,775). In Ohio overall, more than 106,000 provisional ballots were left uncounted, and to this day have never been tallied or accounted for.

- Irregularities in New Mexico paralleled those in Ohio. In a conference call, Kerry later complained that he lost every precinct in New Mexico where ballots were counted by machine rather than by hand. But he never made a public statement to that effect or demanded a recount.

- In Franklin County, where inner city precincts were shorted on voting machines, the turnout among African-Americans was officially 10% lower than in white precincts.

- A post-election study showed it took African-Americans 55 minutes to vote in Ohio 2004 but it took white citizens an average of just 5 minutes

- A door-to-door survey of the Concord Southwest precinct (Ohio) after the 2004 election confirmed that 25 citizens, who were listed as having voted, told the survey team that they actually never did vote in the presidential election. In that precinct, 679 out of the registered 689 voters allegedly cast ballots, according to the Board of Elections, but only 549 actually signed-in to vote. The Board of Elections admitted there had been 130 "phantom votes" and that the vast majority of them had been awarded to Bush.

- In Cuyahoga County at least 8,099 of 24,472 provisional ballots were thrown in the trash.

- In Montgomery County (Dayton) 2.8% of the ballots cast in pro-Kerry precincts showed no vote for president, versus 1.6% in pro-Bush precincts.

- Mathematician Richard Charnin analyzed the 2004 presidential election and found what he calls the "Bush Urban Legend." To accept George W. Bush's 2004 alleged victory, one must accept data that shows Bush's votes declining in rural Republican areas but increasing in Democratic urban areas of the country.

- Michael Collins, writing for Scoop.com, questioned how Bush received 2.5 million fewer rural Republican votes in the 2004 election, compared to the 2000 election, but gained an unexpected 12 point jump from the urban Latino vote across the nation in that same election, according to the national exit polls.

- On September 25, 2006, as result of the *King-Lincoln-Bronzeville* lawsuit, *the Free Press* reported the following additional irregularities in the 2004 election:

- In Delaware County Precinct Genoa I, researcher Stuart Wright viewed and recounted three separate bundles of ballots. In the second bundle, there were 274 consecutive ballots allegedly cast for Bush. In the third bundle there were 359 consecutive ballots allegedly cast for Bush. Genoa I was not one of the four precincts recounted as part of a required official recount, conducted by Blackwell on December 15, 2004.

- In Delaware County, BOE officials told researcher Richard Hayes Phillips that after the votes were cast on Election Day, ballots were unloaded by a team of teenage volunteers including the Boy Scouts who carried them into the BOE building, where they were then given to a "mentally retarded man" who scraped the chads off the punch card ballots. Dr. Phillips estimates that the "mentally retarded man" would have had to scrape four or five ballots per second on election night in order to comply with the posting of the results at 12:40am for the nearly 80,000 ballots cast there.

- In Delaware County, Ross Township precinct, Philips discovered that the BOE certified that 70% of the ballots cast for C. Ellen Connally, an African-American woman from Cleveland running for the Ohio Supreme Court, were also counted for Bush. The implausibility of this outcome in a white, Republican suburb is underscored by the fact that Connally trailed both Bush and Kerry very substantially throughout the rest of the state. Some 60% of the Township's ballots opposing a constitutional amendment banning gay marriage (which passed substantially) also were punched for Bush, an extremely implausible outcome given his opposition to gay marriage. This "anomaly" was widely branded as the "Gays for Bush" phenomenon.

- In Butler County, Phillips found that in Monroe City precinct 4CA, Bush received 52 consecutive votes near the start of voting, and then another run of 212 consecutive votes.

- Also in Butler Country, in Ross Township Precinct 4JB, Philips found that Bush was awarded 547 votes to Kerry's 141 votes. In separate sequences, Bush received 41, 29 and 25 straight votes. Neither 4CA nor 4JB were involved in the official recount.

- In Clermont County, which contributed significantly to Bush's margin of victory, statistical researcher Dr. Ronald Baiman discovered a suspicious use of replacement ballots, meant to be issued only if a regular ballot is somehow spoiled by a voter. In a random draw of ballots as he went through the 192 precincts, against huge odds, Baiman found a replacement ballot. Baiman asked that the next ballot from the precinct be drawn and it, too, was a replacement ballot. Continuing pulling ballots from that same precinct, Baiman witnessed 36 straight replacement ballots in a row, a virtual statistical impossibility. Dr. Philips recorded only five spoiled ballots in this same precinct, raising the question of where the other 31 replacement ballots came from. Both Dr. Philips and Baiman were expert witnesses in the *Moss v. Bush* challenge to the Ohio vote.

- Also in Clermont County, Phillips found an opti-scan ballot with a white sticker over the Kerry-Edwards spot which would prevent the counter from recording a Kerry vote. During the December 2004 recount in Clermont County, witnesses swore in official affidavits that they saw several ballots with stickers over the Kerry-Edwards spot. The county prosecutor claimed there were "less than one hundred" of these, but was unable to explain why any stickers were there at all.

- In Miami County on Monday, June 19, 2006, Director Steve Quillen handed co-author Bob Fitrakis a print out of what he called "freely amended results." Director Quillen said "You guys were right" regarding the voter turnout in Concord South West Precinct, which had been listed as 98.55% in the certified election results in 2004. Quillen also disavowed the alleged 94.3% voter turnout certified election results in Concord South. *The Free Press* has questioned those results, which would have meant that 679 out of 689 people successfully voted in Concord South West. Using a computer databank of voter history, Quillen has since admitted that the voter turnout was just 82.1% in Concord South West and 79.5% in Concord, discrepancies of more than 15%.

- In Miami County, BOE Director Quillen also said Boy Scouts who volunteered to help on Election Day mistakenly took Concord South West ballots to the Concord East precinct. Dr. Ron Baiman, professor and statistician, found that the poll books and absentee ballots in Miami County "have little to no relationship to the voters who voted in the county." He also discovered that "at least 8% of precincts in Miami County have at least a 5% discrepancy between the number of voters who voted and the official certified number of votes." He also noted that there were two precincts that were off by more than 100 votes.

- In Miami County, both the Chair and the Director of the BOE admitted that the recount matched the official vote count only because they didn't use the certified results, but simply counted the ballots in the precinct and ran them through the tabulator. This is a valid tabulator test, but not a legally valid recount, since there's no benchmark.

- Also in Miami County, Diane L. Miley, the BOE's former Deputy Director said the Director allowed "Republican friends" and "high school students to take ballots out to the polls on Election Day." Miley also says ten or more Republicans were allowed into the BOE on the evening of Election Day, when votes were being counted, which she says made her "incredibly uncomfortable." But in going public with her assertions, Miley says she was "abandoned by the Dems . . . when I stood up [to the Republicans] at the Board of Elections."

- In Warren County, punch card ballots were also shifted from precinct to precinct, which again, due to ballot rotations, could have reversed the intent of thousands of voters. Warren County was also key to the Bush margin of victory.

- General disorganization and administrative problems led to the forced resignation of the entire GOP-dominated Board of Elections in Lucas County (Toledo) following the election.

Electronic Election Theft Since 2004

Overall, the electronic dominance of registration records, casting and counting of votes has stripped the public of the ability to verify how Ohio or the country as a whole actually voted in 2004.

We will never know the actual vote count in a national election that resulted in a second term for George W. Bush.

If ever there was a doubt about the ability of a Secretary of State to manipulate an election by electronic means, Florida 2000 and Ohio

2004 should have put it permanently to rest.

Since 2004, the situation has gotten far worse.

The rise of grassroots election integrity organizations all over the country has fed an attempt to monitor the examples of election theft in every election since 2004.

But, should the 2016 election be conducted the day you read this, you will have no expectation of knowing what really happened.

- In March 2005, a group of university professors at the National Election Data Archive Project released a study suggesting that the 2004 presidential vote count could have been altered. Based on an extensive analysis of election data, their *Final Study of the 2004 Presidential Election Poll Discrepancies* concluded, among other things, that "the required pattern of exit poll participation by Kerry and Bush voters to satisfy the exit poll data defies empirical experience and common sense under any assumed scenario."

- On March 25, 2005, Congressman Bob Ney, Chair of the US House Committee on House Administration held hearings in Columbus, Ohio where Blackwell denied any wrongdoing in the 2004 election. The American Center for Voting Rights, a fake voting rights group which was just established a few days earlier was present. Its representative, a Republican operative named Thor Hearne testified that the real problem was the NAACP bribing people to vote Democratic in return for crack.

- In April 2005, a report by the Montgomery County, Maryland Information Technology Department concluded that as a result of 106 machines freezing in the middle of a vote "Maryland election judges are unable to provide substantial confirmation that the vote was in fact counted." The IT report found that there was a 12% failure rate with the machines on Election Day – 7% failed completely, while 5% were suspect because of the low official vote totals.

- In 2006, the Black Box Voting election integrity organization led by Bev Harris showed in three public demonstrations that the optical scan voting machines used in Florida could be hacked.

- In July 2005, Members of the Progressive Ohio Backbone Campaign traveled to the Hocking County Sheriff's Department on Monday morning, July 11, to file an affidavit of fact alleging criminal conduct by the county's Board of Elections (BOE) Director Lisa Schwartze. According to the affidavit, some 10,000 voter registration documents were illegally shredded in Hocking County by Schwartze's BOE. The Hocking County Sheriff's department and Prosecutor refused to investigate the situation.

- On July 29, 2005, California Secretary of State, Bruce McPherson denied the certification of the Diebold TSx GEMS v. 1.18.22 voting machines in his state. McPherson cited a 10% failure rate due to jammed printers and computer "crashes."

- Following the 2004 election, Ohio's Republican Governor Bob Taft filed a no contest plea on four misdemeanor ethics violations involving illegal gifts from Tom Noe, former chair of the Lucas County (Toledo) Board of Elections. Noe was a leader of the Ohio Republican Party and a major Bush-Cheney donor. In his role as BOE chair he was a key player in numerous irregularities involving shifts of votes from Kerry to Bush in 2004.

- In August 2005, Paul Hackett, an Iraq war veteran and a Democratic candidate for Congress in southwestern Ohio, lost his bid late in the evening of a close election. At 9pm election night, with 88% of the votes counted, Hackett and his Republican opponent were in a virtual dead heat. More than half the ballots in Clermont County, Ohio had been tabulated and reported. But then Clermont County election officials reported a "technical malfunction" with optical scan readers. They blamed the problem on "humidity" which allegedly soaked into the Scantron ballots, making it hard for them to pass through computerized tabulators. Once the problem was "solved," Hackett went down to a definitive defeat. The percentages by which he lost votes after the "glitch" was fixed were far higher than those beforehand. Vote counts were also higher than expected in the strongest GOP precincts.

- On August 5, 2005, the lead plaintiff in the *Moss v. Bush* case, Bill Moss, died unexpectedly after a stroke at age 69.

- On August 25, 2005, Stephanie Tubbs Jones, the Congresswoman who challenged the Ohio's electoral votes going to Bush in the first electoral delegation challenge in Ohio history, died unexpectedly of an aneurysm at age 58.

- In September 2005, the US Government Accountability Office (GAO) issued its report entitled Federal Efforts to Improve Security and Reliability of Electronic Voting Systems Are Underway But Key Activities Need To Be Completed. The GAO found that "some of [the] concerns about electronic voting machines have been realized and have caused problems with recent elections, resulting in the loss and miscount of votes." The GAO report documented eight major security flaws, including:

  - Some electronic voting machines "did not encrypt cast ballots or system audit logs, and it was possible to alter both without being detected." In other words, the GAO confirmed that electronic voting machines provided an open door to flip an entire vote count. More than 800,000 votes were cast in Ohio's 2004 election on electronic voting machines, a total more than six times Bush's official margin of victory.

  - The GAO confirmed that "it was possible to alter the files that define how a ballot looks and works so that the votes for one candidate could be recorded for a different candidate." Numerous sworn statements and affidavits assert that this did happen in Ohio 2004.

  - The GAO confirmed that "vendors installed uncertified versions of voting system software at the local level." Thus election results could be falsified without leaving any evidence of such an action by using altered memory cards.

  - The GAO confirmed that access to the voting network was easily compromised because not all digital recording electronic voting systems (DREs) had supervisory functions password-protected. Thus, access to one machine provided access to the whole network. This critical finding confirmed that rigging the 2004 vote did not require a "widespread conspiracy" but rather the cooperation of a very small number of operatives with the power to tap into the networked machines. These individuals could then change large numbers of votes at will. With 800,000 votes cast on electronic machines in Ohio, flipping the number needed to give Bush a margin of 118,775 could be easily done by just one programmer within a short period of time.

  - The GAO confirmed that access to the voting network was

compromised by repeated use of the same user IDs combined with easily guessed passwords. Thus even relatively amateur hackers could have gained access to and altered the Ohio vote tallies.

- The GAO confirmed that locks protecting access to the system were easily picked and keys were simple to copy, meaning, again, getting into the system was an easy matter, even for amateur hackers.

- The GAO confirmed that one DRE model was shown to have been networked in such a rudimentary fashion that a power failure on one machine would cause the entire network to fail, re-emphasizing the fragility of the system on which the presidency was decided.

- The GAO identified further problems with the security protocols and background screening practices for vendor personnel, confirming still more easy access to the system.

- Prior to elections in November 2005, 41 Ohio counties added new paperless computer touchscreen voting machines.

- On the Ohio ballot in November 2005 was Issue 2, a reformist ballot measure with widespread bi-partisan support. Issue 2 was designed to help Ohioans vote earlier by mail or in person. The usually reliable *Columbus Dispatch* newspaper poll showed Issue 2 passing 59%-33% with 8% undecided. The Republican-leaning Bliss Institute at the University of Akron showed Issue 2 winning by 28 points. But Issue 2 was vehemently opposed by GOP Secretary of State J. Kenneth Blackwell, who ran the election. It lost by an astonishing 65.5%-36.5% margin, involving a shift from poll to official outcome that was a virtual statistical impossibility.

- Issue 3 also had wide bi-partisan support, but was also opposed by Blackwell. It involved campaign finance limits. The *Dispatch* poll showed it winning 61%-25%. The Bliss Institute showed it winning by 22 points. But the official vote count, as reported by Blackwell, showed it being defeated 67%-33%. This constituted an unfathomable 71 point swing from the *Dispatch* poll to the actual results, another virtual statistical impossibility. The vote counts on Issues 2 and 3 were never subjected to an independent recount or audit.

- In December 2005, after an acrimonious board meeting, longtime Diebold CEO Walden O'Dell resigned effective immediately. Diebold supplied most of the software for vote tabulation in Ohio counties in the 2004 election. O'Dell had been on record saying he would "deliver" Ohio's vote to Bush. The resignation came amidst a massive class action lawsuit filed in United States District Court in Ohio against the firm and eight current and former executives for securities fraud, concealment, and insider trading. After much turmoil, Diebold renamed its voting division Premier, was bought by ES&S and the remnants were spun off into the Canadian-based Dominion.

- On December 27, 2005, tests conducted on Diebold's TSx touch-screen voting machine by Emery County, Utah, Clerk Bruce Funk revealed new problems. Funk booted each machine up to check the battery. Some of the machines were marked with little yellow dots. Screen messages indicated most machines had about 25 MB of memory available, but some had only 7 MB of free memory left. One had only 4 MB of available memory. For perspective, the backup election file generated by the Diebold TSx is about 7.9 MB. The problem raised three possibilities:

   1. There might be completely different software in the machines with low memory.

   2. Some machines might contain different external data.

   3. Or, some of the machines might have been delivered with different amounts of installed memory.

- In April 2006, *the Free Press* reported that Ohio Secretary of State J. Kenneth Blackwell, Co-Chair of the Bush-Cheney Re-Election Campaign, revealed that he had owned stock in the Diebold voting machine company. Blackwell tried to award unbid state contracts to Diebold worth millions. A top Republican election official told *the Free Press* that a Diebold operative told him he made a $50,000 donation to Blackwell's "political interests."

- In May 2006, Blackwell was awarded the GOP nomination for Ohio governor in a primary election riddled with voting machine breakdowns. In Franklin (Columbus) and Delaware counties, election officials had to "shut down and recalibrate [machines] throughout the day," according to the *Columbus Dispatch*. The *Dispatch* reported that voting machines recorded votes for wrong candidates. Election officials often use "recalibration" as a code word when machines were reported to be malfunctioning and flipping votes.

- In 2006, Edward Felten, professor of computer science and public affairs at Princeton publicly hacked a Diebold AccuVote TS electronic voting machine.

- In 2006, the *King-Lincoln-Bronzeville* federal lawsuit was filed in court. Co-author Bob Fitrakis was co-counsel and co-author Harvey Wasserman was a plaintiff, the case was a civil action alleging that voters in the 2004 Ohio presidential race were deprived of the right to vote by election officials.

- In September 2006, federal Judge Algernon Marbley delivered a precedent-setting decision preserving the ballots and related from the 2004 election. Such ballots were officially protected by federal law, under lock and key, for 24 months. But Blackwell indicated he might order them destroyed before the protection expired. Instead, Marbley ordered Ohio's 88 county Boards of Election to deliver all materials related to the 2004 election to a repository in Columbus. But when it came time to deliver, 56 of the 88 counties announced their materials were missing. Holmes County officials claimed ballots were destroyed by coffee spilled from a coffee pot. In Mahoning County, the ballots were mistakenly put out to be recycled. No one was prosecuted for the destruction of this public property. At least 114,000 ballots from that election remain uncounted.

- In the Georgia 2006 primary election, US House Representative Cynthia McKinney lost to her opponent Hank Johnson. Voters complained that votes were flipping before their eyes, according to a report on democrats.com by Bob Fertik. He reported: "'You've got electronic voting machines. Many people called in and shared their concern. They pushed the button for Cynthia McKinney and Hank Johnson came up. It wasn't one time, it wasn't two times, it was many, many times,' Karen Fitzpatrick, who has been monitoring elections for US Rep. McKinney's re-election campaign, told *Atlanta Progressive News* in an exclusive interview."

- On May 11, 2006, a security alert from Black Box Voting on Diebold machines noted that "Back doors were found in three separate levels. They can be used one at a time or combined for a deep attack that can permanently compromise the Diebold touch-screens."

- In June 2006, Dr. Ron Baiman, professor and statistician, published an analysis of the so-called "Connelly anomaly" from Ohio's 2004 election. C. Ellen Connally was a Cleveland Democrat running for state Supreme Court. She is African-American. Against all odds, her official vote count somehow ran significantly ahead of Kerry in certain critical heavily-white conservative areas of southwestern Ohio where she did not campaign and had virtually no name recognition. Baiman concluded that the discrepancy indicated an electronic shift of 75,000-82,000 votes from Kerry to Bush.

- In August 2006, a Zogby poll found 92% of Americans demanded the right to watch their votes being counted and 80% rejected the use of secret computer software for vote tabulation.

- On August 16, 2006, Tim Kettler, Green Party candidate for Secretary of State, filed a criminal complaint in Coshocton County, Ohio alleging misconduct in the recount of the 2004 presidential election.

- In September 2006, Dorothy Fadiman's documentary *Stealing America: Vote by Vote* premiered in Columbus, Ohio at the Drexel Theater. Fadiman, an Emmy-award-winning and Oscar-nominated filmmaker, documented the irregularities in the Ohio 2004 election. Local corporate media and local public radio and television stations blacked out the premiere, with virtually no coverage whatsoever on a major documentary made by a nationally-known filmmaker covering substantive allegations that a presidential election was stolen in their own backyard.

- On September 30, 2006, Dr. Ron Baiman, professor and statistician, released a statistical report calling Ohio's 2004 presidential results into question. He revealed an email exchange between himself and expert exit pollster Warren Mitofsky. The report included an email on December 7, 2005, in which Mitofsky responded to Baiman's call for the release of more data with the following phrase: "Go fuck yourself."

- On November 1, 2006, the *Free Press* reported that "Official states electronic voting system added votes never cast in 2004 Presidential election; audit log missing." *The Columbus Free Press* documented in a 17-page report that approximately 2500 votes were added to Miami County's electronic voting system even though they were never cast by actual voters. The audit log for the system was still missing along with all its information for the 2004 presidential election. This was thought to be the first time election officials admitted that computerized cyber-votes not representing real voters were added to a system.

- On November 1, 2006, Ohio Secretary of State Blackwell issued a directive barring from polling places all election observers not authorized by him personally.

- According to Election Data Services, almost 80% of all voters in 2006 voted on electronic voting machines or optically-scanned ballots nationwide. Less than 1% of voters in the U.S. used traditional hand-counted paper ballots.

- In November 2006, the Cuyahoga County Prosecutor filed criminal charges against voting rights activist Victoria Lovegren for passing out data collection forms to election technicians so they could report vote counts for verification. She was officially charged with "obstruction of business."

- On November 7, 2006 in Newtown Square, Pennsylvania, 984 voters cast their ballots in precinct Newtown 1. The voting machine tallied 1089 ballots a 10% overvote.

- On November 14, 2006, Ohio's 2006 vote count included a higher percentage of uncounted ballots than in 2004, and a statistically impossible swing to the Republicans. Nonetheless, Blackwell, who by this time was extremely unpopular with voters, was defeated in a landslide in his race for governor and Democrat Jennifer Brunner became secretary of state.

- On January 2, 2007, the *Free Press* reported that there had been a 26.48% undervote in heavily African-American Cuyahoga County in the Congressional 2006 midterm election. The expected rate of undervotes was approximately 3% statewide.

- On January 3, 2007, the *Free Press* reported massive discrepancies in the Ohio State Auditor's race between 2006 election night reported votes cast and the later official tally. In the Cleveland area, 94,442 votes, a shocking 16.8% of all the votes in Cuyahoga County, disappeared from the official tally. Republican newcomer Mary Taylor, who is white, defeated Democrat Barbara Sykes, who is black, in the Ohio

State Auditor's race. Pre-election polls showed Sykes winning by 10%. (Taylor has since become Ohio's Lieutenant Governor and has announced her intent to run for governor in 2018).

- On January 4, 2007, *Free Press* reporter Rady Ananda reported that 60% of all randomly audited precincts in Franklin County showed that more official votes were tallied in a Franklin County judge's race than there were voters.

- On January 27, 2007, the first felony convictions were handed down against two Cleveland poll workers stemming from Ohio's 2004 presidential election recount. Cuyahoga County prosecutors say the poll workers "rigged" the recount.

- On February 6, 2007, Michael Vu, Director of the Cuyahoga County Board of Elections, resigned over his handling of Ohio's 2004 election and official recount.

- On March 6, 2007, a third Cuyahoga County Board of Elections official was found guilty of rigging the 2004 Ohio recount. Also, a recount of the Coshocton County presidential votes raised Kerry's total from the officially reported 43% to 49%.

- On March 26, 2007, the *Free Press* reported that a court affidavit claimed that Michael Barbian, Jr. of Triad Governmental Systems, Inc. left a message to the Hocking County Board of Elections saying he would be in, just prior to the Ohio 2004 recount, "to check out your tabulator and computer…" Triad's management and ownership are tied to the Republican Party and the Right to Life movement. There was no appointment to inspect the Hocking County BOE's equipment prior to the recount day.

- On June 21, 2007, Senator John Edwards became the first major presidential candidate to support "open source code" for U.S. elections. In a letter, Edwards stated that "To ensure security, these machines should be programmed with an open source code for complete transparency, and election results should be safeguarded by voter-verified paper records." As John Kerry's running mate, Edwards had vehemently objected to Kerry's early concession of the presidential race before all votes were counted in Ohio.

- On December 7, 2007, Ohio Secretary of State Jennifer Brunner announced that a $1.9 million official study, entitled *Everest*, showed that "critical security failures" were embedded throughout the voting systems in the state that decided the 2004 election. Those failures, she said, "could impact the integrity of elections in the Buckeye State." They have rendered Ohio's vote counts "vulnerable" to manipulation and theft by "fairly simple techniques."

- In January 2008, the *Free Press* published an article detailing the *Voting Industrial Complex* establishing long-standing ties between the Republican Party, the Federal Election Commission and officials at the major voting machine companies.

- In Ohio's March 2008 primary, at least 15 touch-screen voting machines that produced improbable numbers in Ohio's 2006 statewide election were under double-lock in an official crime scene, following an order from Ohio Secretary of State Jennifer Brunner, after her husband witnessed discrepancies on the electronic ballots.

- Investigative reporter Greg Palast revealed that in the 2008 Presidential election, 1,451,116 ballots were "spoiled," not counted nationally – and 54% of those were cast by African-Americans.

- The whistleblower, Stephen Spoonamore, who has run or held senior technology positions in six technology companies, and whose clients have included MasterCard, American Express, NBC-GE, and federal agencies including the State Department and the Navy, said Mike Connell, a longtime Republican Party computer networking contractor, "agrees that the electronic voting systems in the US are not secure" and told Spoonamore in 2007 "that he (Connell) is afraid some of the more ruthless partisans of the GOP may have exploited systems he in part worked on for this purpose."

- Various threats were repeatedly reported involving Michael Connell and other IT experts close to the GOP. On July 24, 2008, Arnebeck emailed US Attorney General Michael Mukasey, stating: "We have been confidentially informed by a source we believe to be credible that Karl Rove has threatened Michael Connell, a principal witness we have identified in our *King-Lincoln* case in federal court in Columbus, Ohio...."

- On Monday, November 3, 2008, one day before national elections, under federal deposition questioning by attorneys Cliff Arnebeck and Bob Fitrakis, Michael Connell revealed that while under contract with the State of Ohio to tabulate the 2004 presidential vote count, he was working with SmartTech, the private contractor in charge of Karl Rove's personal email server, as well as the GOP's national website and the Bush-Cheney campaign's website, and with Triad, which had fixed the official 2004 recount. Essentially this meant that the vote count that decided the 2004 presidential outcome was done in conjunction with a private Republican-sponsored IT firm with no independent verification. Connell was informed that he would be called again to be deposed after further discovery. Connell remained the IT supervisor for six Congressional committees.

- On Friday, December 19, 2008, five weeks after being deposed, and after being informed he would be deposed again, computer expert Michael Connell, age 45, was killed in a mysterious single-engine plane crash. An expert pilot, Connell died while flying his Piper Saratoga plane home to Akron, Ohio in unremarkable weather from College Park, Maryland. Connell's family has since raised questions about his death, questioning the official story that his crash was the result of pilot error. The FBI took over the crash site from the FAA and cleaned up the scene overnight, rather than wait for daylight. Mike Connell's cell phone was officially never found. Connell's unexplained death marked a major set-back in the process of uncovering what really happened in Ohio 2004.

- On March 25, 2009, a new *Free Press* study revealed that more than a million Ohio voters were purged in run up to 2008 election and that the Republican Party had wanted still another 800,000 voters purged.

- On September 3, 2009, the ES&S voting machine company purchased Premier Voting, formerly known as Diebold, giving ES&S control of an estimated 80% of the electronic voting market in the U.S.

- In November 2009, Ohio Secretary of State Jennifer Brunner held an Election Summit summarizing the 2008 presidential election. Professor Ted Allen of Ohio State University, an expert in "waiting line analysis theory," said that voters using voting machines on average took two minutes longer than those voting on paper. He also pointed out that had Franklin County used the same number of voting machines in 2008 as they did in 2004, the wait would have been "30 hours." Without early voting in Ohio, the voter wait in 2008 would have been, on average, 15 hours.

- In 2010, computer scientist J. Alex Halderman of the University of Michigan participated in an open-to-the-public to hack into an experimental Internet voting system created in DC for overseas voters, including military. Halderman and some grad students, within 24 hours, totally tore the system apart, ending it with the UMich fight song to signal to voters that their process had been successfully "completed."

- In August 2010, Ohio Secretary of State Jennifer Brunner sued Diebold alleging that the company's voting machines "dropped votes in at least 11 counties" in the 2008 presidential primary. Diebold settled the lawsuit by offering discounted voting machines to the counties in question.

- In September 2010, Bev Harris of Black Box Voting reported that an election audit of Shelby County, Tennessee found 3221 phantom votes from voters who were never signed in to vote.

- In October 2010, Black Box Voting reported that two former felons, embezzler Jeffrey Dean and narcotics trafficker John Elder, received a contract from King County (Seattle) Washington to computerize the county's vote-by-mail program. At the time of the award, King County had approximately one million voters, with some 600,000 voting absentee.

- In Ohio's 2010 gubernatorial race, exit polls showed GOP challenger John Kasich as having lost to incumbent Democrat Ted Strickland. Kasich received a $1,000,000.00 check from media baron Rupert Murdoch just before the election. The official vote count showed Kasich the winner.

- Also in Ohio 2010, the GOP challenger for Attorney General, former US Senator Mike DeWine, also lost in the exit polls but won in the official vote count against the current Attorney General, Richard Cordray.

- In March 2011, the Ohio Republican-dominated legislature passed HB 159, targeting 900,000 mostly Democratic and minority voters for disenfranchisement. The bill allowed the acceptance of only four types of picture ID to vote – a U.S. passport, a U.S. military ID, an Ohio driver's license, or an Ohio state ID – making it one of the most restrictive in the nation.

- On July 20, 2011, the *Free Press* obtained and published an election contract signed with GovTech, Michael Connell's private IT company that allowed the 2004 Ohio electronic vote count to be stolen, plus a graphic architectural map of the Secretary of State's election night server layout system linked to the IT site in Tennessee. Both documents were filed in the *King Lincoln Bronzeville v. Blackwell* case.

- Following the November 2011 election in Franklin County, Ohio, Board of Elections officials in Columbus admitted that "programming errors" had prevented "many precincts" from being able to print out their vote totals to display at polling sites. This was in violation of Ohio law, which requires all precinct results be posted for display after the polls close on Election Day.

- On December 22, 2011, the U.S. Election Assistance Commission (EAC) issued a formal investigative report on Election Systems & Software (ES&S) DS200 Precinct County optical scanners. The EAC ruled that the ballot scanners made by ES&S electronic voting machine firm failed 10% of the time to read the votes correctly. The EAC found "three substantial anomalies":

  - Intermittent screen freezes, system lock-ups and shutdowns that prevent the voting system from operating in the manner in which it was designed.

  - Failure to log all normal and abnormal voting system events.

  - Skewing of the ballot resulting in a negative effect on system accuracy.

- Obama's popular vote should have been higher in 2008, according to mathematician Richard Charnin, and analysts Francois Choquette and James Johnson. They discovered a statistical anomaly that awards Republicans with a higher number of votes than expected based on pre-election polls and exit polls. In September 2012, Choquette and Johnson published a ground-breaking statistical report. Their analysis in the report *2008-2012 Election Anomalies, Results, Analysis and Concerns* showed how Romney inexplicably gained votes in larger precincts when running in primary elections and only when voters are counted by computers. This was true for Romney in the 2008 primary, the 2012 primaries, and general election.

- Dr. Beth Clarkson, a Wichita State statistician, found the same pattern as Choquette and Johnson in the 2012 Ohio presidential election, the 2014 Wisconsin gubernatorial election, and the Kansas Senate election that year. Clarkson sued her county board of elections commission when they refused to allow her to audit the county's 2014 voting paper trial.

- On April 15, 2012, the *Free Press* obtained public records from all 88 Ohio county Boards of Elections (BOE) documenting that 1,092,392 voters were removed from the voting rolls since the previous presidential election in 2008. Cuyahoga County (Cleveland) led the Buckeye State with 267,071 purges. Franklin County (Columbus) removed 93,578 voters. Franklin County went 58% for Obama in the 2008 election. Hamilton County (Cincinnati) removed 65,536 voters, for a total of 426,185 from these three heavily Democratic Ohio counties. Heavily Republican rural Ohio counties including Hancock, Huron, Sandusky, and Wood, reported no purges at all.

- On October 24, 2012, in the lead-up to the presidential election, the *Free Press* reported that through a closely held equity fund called Solamere, Mitt Romney and his wife, son and brother were major investors in an investment firm called H.I.G. Capital. H.I.G. in turn held a majority share (three out of the five board members) on Hart Intercivic, whose voting machines were being used in the 2012 election in heavily populated Hamilton County (Cincinnati). Hamilton County was expected to be a key to the outcome of the election in Ohio.

- On October 31, 2012, the *Free Press* learned that ES&S installed "experimental" software patches on voting machines in as many as 39 Ohio counties affecting 4,041,056 registered voters, including those in metropolitan Columbus and Cleveland (www.verifiedvoting.org) , involving as much as 80% of the Ohio vote count. The contract called for ES&S technicians and county poll workers to "enter custom codes and interfaces" to the standard election reporting software just as was done with the controversial 2004 Ohio presidential election.

- On November 2, 2012, the *Free Press* obtained internal memos from the senior staff of the Ohio Secretary of State's office confirming the installation of untested and uncertified election tabulation software in the apparatus counting the votes in the upcoming election.

- On November 5, 2012 the *Free Press* revealed invoices that proved Romney-related voting company Hart InterCivic did key maintenance on Cincinnati's voting machines. Amy Searcy, Hamilton County Board of Elections director of elections, falsely told the *Cincinnati Enquirer* and the *Washington Post* that Hart InterCivic was not involved with operations or maintenance of their voting machines in Hamilton County. But her signature was on a quote from Hart InterCivic for voting machine repair. One of the invoices from Hart InterCivic to Hamilton County was for $134,125.00 worth of ballots; another was for $15,386.40 worth of maintenance services.

- On the day before Election Day 2012, *Free Press* Editor Bob Fitrakis sued Ohio Secretary of State Jon Husted over the "experimental" software patches places on electronic voting machines in 44 Ohio counties and the Secretary of State's office. Fitrakis also challenged an unbid non-public contract granted to ES&S to install the experimental patches. Republican-appointed Federal Court Judge Frost denied a temporary restraining order on Election Day. Fitrakis immediately went to Ohio's Common Pleas Court to file the same suit before a sympathetic judge who allowed the case to remain open until the final election results were certified. Judge Serrott indicated that he would allow the case to go forward if there were "funny numbers" in the election.

- On November 6, 2012, as Obama was re-elected to the presidency, the tabulation website run by Ohio Secretary of State (now Republican Jon Husted) went down at 11:13 pm. At 12:23am on Election Day morning, Forbes.com posted a lengthy report on America's shaky electronic voting technology and how it might be used to tamper with votes in the United States' foremost swing state.

- On election night, 2012, Karl Rove had his infamous meltdown on Fox News. As election results from Ohio were coming in showing Obama winning the state, Rove continually insisted that there would be a miraculous comeback by Romney. But, as the results proceeded to prove him wrong, he lost it on camera, becoming a viral online video the next day.

- On November 16, 2012, the *Free Press* published its account of the 2012 presidential election entitled, *Why Rove failed to deliver Ohio on Election Day: What happened in Ohio* – this time around. The Ohio Secretary of State's vote tabulation website went down at 11:13pm, as reported by *Free Press* election protection website monitors, and mentioned by Rove on the news. When the *Free Press* investigated Bush's implausible 2004 victory in Ohio, it was discovered that ES&S and Triad technicians had placed similar last-minute unauthorized patches on tabulators in various Ohio counties including Miami and Clermont.

- On January 31, 2013, Lou Dubose wrote an article in the *Washington Spectator* entitled, *Did an Election Day Lawsuit Stop Karl Rove's Vote-Rigging Scheme in Ohio?* He suggested that the last minute 2012 Election Day lawsuit regarding the experimental patched on vote tabulators in Ohio filed by Cliff Arnebeck, with co-author Bob Fitrakis as the Plaintiff, helped prevent a stolen election for Romney in Ohio.

- In June 2013, the US Supreme Court "…effectively struck down the heart of the Voting Rights Act of 1965 by a 5-to-4 vote, freeing nine states, mostly in the South, to change their election laws without advance federal approval," according to the *New York Times*.

- On October 22, 2013, federal prosecutors filed charges against Diebold, Inc. The company had bribed government officials and falsified documents to obtain business in China, Indonesia and Russia.

- In December 2013, the *Free Press* reported on a crucial document that shed light on Connell's mysterious death, as the fifth anniversary of his tragic accident approached. The document revealed that then-Ohio Secretary of State J. Kenneth Blackwell had signed a legal Statement of Work (SOW) contract fourteen months prior to the 2004 election with Connell's company GovTech. The contract stated that Connell would have "remote monitoring capabilities" to the computers counting Ohio's presidential vote.

- On October 2, 2014, the *Free Press* published an article revealing how Ohio's Republican Secretary of State Jon Husted was poised to accumulate all real time voting data in the state without the media being able to see it simultaneously. The next day, Husted reversed the policy.

- On October 9, 2014, the *Free Press* published an article outlining how electronic poll books undermine security of elections and secrecy of the ballot by allowing voters names to be linked to their electronic vote and allowing remote access to the voter rolls.

- On November 7, 2014, the *Free Press* reported on the ability of a secretive election company, Scytl, to manipulate election results through its state-of-the-art software. Scytl counts the overseas vote and has been given access to central vote tabulators in a majority of states.

- Mathematician Richard Charnin demonstrated, with three different mathematical models, that it was likely that three gubernatorial elections were stolen in 2014: Maine, Michigan and Oregon. Serious questions have also been raised about that year's US Senate races in North Carolina, Alaska and Colorado, where dubious Republican victories gave the GOP definitive control of the Upper House.

- In March 2015, the Harvard Electoral Integrity Project reported that over fourteen hundred international election experts gathered data the year before and pronounced the United States was 45th in election integrity among the world's long-standing democracies. The Project reported that on a 100-point scale, the U.S. received an integrity rating of 69.3% – one notch ahead of the narco-drug state Colombia at 69.1% and just behind the nearly-narco-drug state of Mexico at 69.8%, neither country with a long-standing democracy.

- In 2015, one of the Princeton computer scientists who successfully hacked voting machines, Edward William Felten, was appointed Deputy U.S. Chief Technology Officer by President Obama.

- On November 3, 2015, Ohio's Issue 3 marijuana legalization issue went up in smoke. Pre-election tracking polls showed it winning by a margin of 65-35%.

- The proposition was vehemently opposed by GOP Governor John Kasich (who has repeatedly admitted to smoking pot himself), Secretary of State Jon Husted and numerous other top Republican officials.

- Screenshots from election night vote tallies on media websites showed the issue actually winning 65%-35% with 39% of the votes reporting, in line with pre-election tracking polls. But just moments later, with just 9% more of the vote coming in, it flipped to 65%-35% officially in opposition. Dr. Ron Baiman, professor and statistician called the outcome "a virtual statistical impossibility."

- Statistician Dr. Beth Clarkson's work noted that in certain elections, Democratic candidates seemed to benefit from vote flipping. In 2016, Josh Mitteldorf pointed out that the exit polls strongly suggested that Bernie Sanders had won Massachusetts, but the official result gave the state implausibly to Hillary Clinton. The unadjusted exit polls showed Sanders winning 52-46 over Clinton. The actual vote count showed Clinton barely squeaking by 50-49. This seven-point disparity in the exit polls – the gold standard for indicating election fraud worldwide – should have caused a major scandal in the United States. Many political commentators felt that if Clinton lost to Sanders in Massachusetts it would shift her to an underdog position in the primary race.

- Major irregularities have also called into question the 2015 race for governor of Kentucky, an extreme right-wing Tea Party fanatic won in an unexpected landslide, with no meaningful recount. The new governor's first act was to reinstate laws disenfranchising tens of thousands of Kentucky citizens.

- As of this writing, the 2016 primaries have already been marred by voting machine shortages, elimination of precincts and long lines, resulting in mass disenfranchisement, in Arizona and Wisconsin. In Latino areas of Arizona voters stood in line for five hours and more.

- The advent of Jim Crow-style photo ID and other restrictive registration laws indicate massive intentional disenfranchisement through the 2016 primaries and into the general election. Fitrakis and Palast have estimated hundreds of thousands of disenfranchised voters in Ohio alone. The ACLU of Ohio sued Secretary of State Jon Husted for purging two million voters from the voting rolls in the run-up to the election.

- *The New York Times* and others have estimated some some 300,000 citizens were stripped of their right to vote in the Wisconsin primary by photo ID and other laws. More Republicans were reported as having voted in that primary than Democrats, with the margin likely to carry through the fall general election, thanks to the mass disenfranchisement.

- In fall, 2016, more than half the ballots in the general election will be cast on electronic voting machines whose tallies cannot be independently verified. In swing states like Florida, North Carolina,

Ohio, Michigan, Iowa and Arizona, among others, Republican governors will have the opportunity to swing the electronic vote count without public disclosure or accountability.

- In the fall 2016 election, most of the nation's electronic voting machines will have been purchased with funds from the Help America Vote Act of 2002, making them a decade or more in age, and highly vulnerable to even amateur hackers.

- Because court rulings still protect voting machine manufacturers, there will be no meaningful way to monitor or confirm the veracity of the vote count in the 2016 presidential race, or in those for the US Congress, governorships, statehouses and virtually all other elected offices in the United States.

Distrust of 2016's hackable election is a media landslide with just one solution: Hand-counted paper ballots

Finally, the major for-profit media is approaching consensus that it's easy to hack U.S. political elections. Even candidates Hillary Clinton and Donald Trump are raising unprecedented doubts – from very different directions – about the reliability of the upcoming vote count.

Ultimately, there is just one solution: universal hand-counted paper ballots, with carefully protected voter registration rolls, and a transparent chain of custody.

The corporate media and the Democrats are obsessed with the "Russians." Donald Trump rants about a mythological army of voters voting multiple times.

But the real threat to our election system comes from private for-profit corporations that register voters, control voter databases, then count and report the vote with secret proprietary software and zero transparency, accountability, or recourse.

After ignoring or attacking the reportage since Florida 2000 of Bev Harris, Greg Palast, *freepress.org* and numerous others, the corporate media seems finally to be getting the message: under the current system, any American election – even the one for president – can be stripped and flipped by a tiny handful of electronic hackers working anywhere from the Kremlin to a party HQ to a state governor's office to a teenager's garage.

Here is some of what the mainstream media is finally admitting.

In an article posted on July 28, 2016, *NBC News* pointed out that our elections are vulnerable to hacking because they "are not part of the vast 'critical infrastructure protection' safety net set up by the Department of Homeland Security."

CBS News wrote August 10, 2016, about "the hackers at Symantec Security Response" who demonstrated how "Election Day results could be manipulated by an affordable device you can find online.

Former national coordinator for counter-terrorism Richard Clarke, reporting for *ABC News* on August 19, 2016, analyzed the particular security problems related to battleground states like Ohio and Florida: "In 2000 and 2004, there were only a handful of battleground states that determined which presidential candidate had enough Electoral College votes to win. A slight alteration of the vote in some swing precincts in swing states might not raise suspicion. Smart malware can be programmed to switch only a small percentage of votes from what the voters intended. That may be all that is needed, and that malware can also be programmed to erase itself after it does its job, so there might be no trace it ever happened." Clarke was on the White House National Security Council during both Bill Clinton's and George W. Bush's administrations.

Zeynep Tufekci, an associate professor at the North Carolina School of Information and Library Science, in his August 12, 2016 *New York Times* op-ed "The Election Won't Be Rigged but It Could Be Hacked," wrote: "The mere existence of this discussion is cause for alarm. The United States needs to return, as soon as possible, to a paper-based, auditable voting system in all jurisdictions that still use electronic-only, unverifiable voting machines."

On August 30, 2016, the *Washington Post* wrote: "Deleting or altering data on voter rolls could cause mayhem on Election Day disenfranchising some voters. Many voting machines themselves also are vulnerable, especially touch-screen systems that do not create a paper record as a guard against fraud or manipulation." The Post also supplied a list of the 15 states with the most vulnerable voting systems.

The list of those now admitting the obvious includes the *Boston Globe, The Atlantic, USA Today, The Guardian, Mother Jones,* and *Politico,* some of which have previously mocked those of us reporting on this issue. Most important has been the highly influential *The Hill,* which weighed in on May 2, 2016 with "Election fraud feared as hackers target voter records." The lede was straightforward: "A series of data breaches overseas are spurring concerns that hackers could manipulate elections in the United States."

Trump advisor Roger Stone wrote a column in *The Hill* with the headline: "Can the 2016 Elections Be Rigged? You Bet." He also referred to our latest summary volume, "The Strip & Flip Selection of 2016: Five Jim Crows & Electronic Election Theft," as "a must-read book on the strip and flip techniques used to rig these machines."

But in the 2016 primary election, there are other must-reads as well. Perhaps the most important is *Election Justice USA*'s report entitled "Democracy Lost: A Report on the Fatally Flawed 2016 Democratic Primaries." This report cites six major areas of election irregularities in this year's 26 primary elections:

1) Targeting voter suppression
2) Registration tampering
3) Illegal voter purges
4) Exit poll discrepancies
5) Evidence for voting machine tampering
6) The security (or lack thereof) of various voting machines types.

In their 96-page report, *Election Justice* researchers documented how Hillary Clinton's campaign benefited from these "various types of fraud." Their conclusion: "Based on this work, Election Justice USA has established an upper estimate of 184 pledged delegates lost by Senator Bernie Sanders as a consequence of specific irregularities and instances of fraud."

Election Justice's well-documented estimate that Sanders lost 184 delegates means that if the election had been conducted fairly, the Senator from Vermont would now be the Democratic nominee.

Another document essential to understanding election irregularities that allowed Hillary Clinton to capture the Democratic Party nomination is a paper co-authored by Axel Geijsel of Tilburg University in the Netherlands and Rodolfo Cortes Barragan of Stanford University. Their analysis found that primary election results in states with the most vulnerable and hackable voting machines and without a paper trail overwhelmingly favored Hillary Clinton 65 percent to 35 percent. Sanders led Clinton 51 percent to 49 percent in states where the vote count could be verified with a paper trail.

The correlation between the increased Clinton vote and the increased vulnerability of the voting machines has been avoided like the plague by the corporate media.

Equally important to read is mathematician Richard Charnin's blog. Charnin is a man the mainstream media often attacks – but not with mathematical formulas to rebut Charnin's detailed analysis. Rather they attack him because, like the vast majority of Americans, he believes that John F. Kennedy was not killed by a lone gunman. In 2016, official Democratic primary vote counts compared to exit poll results were significantly outside the margin of error in 12 of 26 states. Charnin concluded that the probability of those official vote tallies being correct are one in 78 billion. There were no such discrepancies in this year's Republican primaries.

Now 16 years after the theft of the presidency in Florida 2000, and a dozen since it was done again in Ohio 2004, the corporate media are approaching consensus that it is indeed very easy to strip millions of legitimate citizens from the voting rolls, and then to hack electronic voting machines and computerized central tabulators to flip the official final outcome.

The threat to this year's election does not come from non-existent armies of mythological hordes voting multiple times. It comes from the private partisan companies with their secret proprietary software that control the voter rolls, the electronic machines, and ultimately the final outcome at all levels of government. The mega-corporations are the ones that flipped George W. Bush into the White House and Hillary Clinton into the Democratic nomination, not to mention manipulating countless Senate, House, and state and local elections along the way.

For a hopelessly vulnerable electronic election system which is flawed, hackable and riggable from top to bottom, there is just one solution: transparent unhackable voter rolls, and universal hand-counted paper ballots open to public scrutiny from the precinct level to the final official tallies, as dutifully reported by our slowly awakening corporate media.

Afterword

As we approach the 2016 election, the prospects for a truly democratic outcome are grim.

We face devastating crises of corporate domination, social injustice, military madness and ecological catastrophe. The only cure is a bottom-up revolution in human consciousness and action.

But the Jim Crow restrictions on our purported democracy have been with us a long time. Once again, in revised modern form, they've swept through the nation's electoral system like a plague.

The electronic voting machines that will record more than half the nation's votes are mostly a decade old, easily hackable and controlled in numerous key swing states by secretaries of state and governors that can manipulate the official outcome.

We hope the preceding compendium of facts on the corrupted nature of our electoral system will help inform and motivate an energized grassroots uprising.

In the long run, only an enlightened human consciousness can cure our ills. Only a bottom-up movement can save our species.

Time is short. Let's do it.

(By way of disclosure, Bob Fitrakis and Harvey Wasserman are both affiliated with the Green Party).

About Bob Fitrakis and Harvey Wasserman

Bob Fitrakis and Harvey Wasserman witnessed election suppression in Ohio's 2004 presidential election. Subsequently, Fitrakis was one of four attorneys to file the *Moss v. Bush* challenge to Ohio's presidential elections results and Wasserman was one of the plaintiffs in the case. In 2006, Fitrakis was co-counsel and Wasserman was a plaintiff, in the *King-Lincoln-Bronzeville* lawsuit against the Ohio

Secretary of State's office seeking to end racially discriminatory electoral practices in Ohio and to ensure free and fair elections. The two authored a 50-point consent decree to ensure election integrity in Ohio submitted to the current Secretary of State. Many of these proposals have been adopted by the state of Ohio. Both briefed the Congressional Progressive Caucus in 2005.

In the meantime, Fitrakis and Wasserman co-authored hundreds of articles exposing the election fraud of Ohio's 2004 election and subsequent elections all over the country, including one that was chosen for a Project Censored award in 2005: *How a Republican Election Supervisor Manipulated the 2004 Central Ohio Vote.* Fitrakis is the editor of the *Free Press*, freepress.org and columbusfreepress. com. Wasserman is the Senior Editor of freepress.org. Their investigative reporting at www.freepress.org prompted Rev. Jesse Jackson to call them "the Woodward and Bernstein of the 2004 election."

Fitrakis and Wasserman have co-authored several books: *Impeach Bush, George w. Bush vs. The Superpower of Peace, Did George W. Bush Steal America's 2004 Election? Ohio's Essential Documents* (with Steve Rosenfeld), *How the GOP stole America's 2004 election and is rigging 2008, What Happened in Ohio: A documentary record of theft and fraud in the 2004 election* (with Steve Rosenfeld), *As Goes Ohio: Election Theft Since 2004* and *Corporate Vote Theft & the Future of American Democracy* (with Gerry Bello). They have appeared on countless news shows and in independent documentaries about election integrity.

Bob Fitrakis

Fitrakis is a Political Science Professor in the Social Sciences department at Columbus State Community College, where he won the Distinguished Professor Award in 2012. He has a Ph.D. in Political Science from Wayne State University and a J.D. from The Ohio State University Moritz College of Law. As a journalist, Fitrakis has won eleven investigative journalism awards from the Cleveland Press Club, Project Censored, and the Ohio Society of Professional Journalists.

Fitrakis has been an election protection activist since March 1994, when he served as an international observer for the national elections in El Salvador. He co-wrote and edited the El Salvador election report for the United Nations. Fitrakis was an election protection attorney on November 2, 2004 in Franklin County. In December 2004, Fitrakis testified before the Judiciary Committee of Congress at the request of Rep. John Conyers in both Washington D.C. and Columbus. The information gathered from the Fitrakis' investigations and hearings resulted in the Conyers Report, *What Went Wrong in Ohio?* released January 5, 2005. Fitrakis briefed John Kerry, worked on election reform with Rep. Maxine Waters (D-LA), and briefed the Democratic Party Senate leadership. Dr. Fitrakis testified at the Election Assessment hearings in Houston, Texas in 2005, which became part of the Carter-Baker Commission Report on federal election reform. He has also briefed the Senate Democratic leadership, as well as briefing the Congressional Black Caucus in 2005 and 2016.

Harvey Wasserman

Wasserman has taught history, cultural diversity, globalization and journalism at Columbus State Community College, Capital University and Hampshire College. He holds an MA in US history from the University of Chicago and a BA from the University of Michigan.

Wasserman is a life-long activist, teacher, radio host and author or co-author of a dozen books including *SOLARTOPIA! Our Green-Powered Earth*, *Harvey Wasserman's History of the U.S.*. and, *A Glimpse of the Big Light: Losing Parents, Finding Spirit*. With wind pioneer Dan Juhl, Harvey co-authored *Harvesting Wind Energy as a Cash Crop: A Guide to Community-Owned Wind Farming* (www. danmar.us).

In 1968 Wasserman helped found the legendary anti-war Liberation News Service, and the communal/organic Montague (Massachusetts) Farm, now a conference center. In 1973 he helped pioneer the global grassroots movement against atomic reactors, then helped organize mass demonstrations at Seabrook, N.H., and New York City's 1979 "No Nukes" concerts and rally, featuring Bruce Springsteen, Bonnie Raitt, Jackson Browne, CSN, James Taylor and others.

Wasserman's *Green Power & Wellness Show* currently runs on progressiveradionetwork.com. His appearances throughout the major media and at concerts, campus and grassroots citizen gatherings have focused since the 1960s on energy, environment, peace, justice, U.S. history and election protection. In 1994 he spoke to 350,000 semi-conscious rock fans at Woodstock II.

With Bonnie Raitt, Jackson Browne, Graham Nash and others, Wasserman helped found NukeFree.org, which helped stop a $50 billion federal loan guarantee program proposed by the US reactor industry in fall, 2007.